THE TEACHER'S
IDEA BOOK SERIES

"I Know What's Next!"

Preschool Transitions Without Tears or Turmoil

THE TEACHER'S IDEA BOOK SERIES

"I Know What's Next!"

Preschool Transitions Without Tears or Turmoil

Betsy Evans

HIGHSCOPE PRESS®

Ypsilanti, Michigan

Published by

High/Scope® Press
A division of the High/Scope Educational Research Foundation
600 North River Street
Ypsilanti, Michigan 48198-2898
(734)485-2000, fax (734)485-0704
press@highscope.org

Editors: Nancy Altman Brickman, Marcella Weiner
Illustrations: Heather Sky Fulton
Cover and text design: Judy Seling of Seling Design

Photos:

Betsy Evans: 2, 4, 13, 14 (top left & right), 16, 32, 33, 39 (top left & right), 47, 48, 51, 57, 59, 61 (top), 67, 70, 75 (top left & bottom), 76, 77, 78, 82, 87, 88 (top), 89 (top & center), 95

Devon Evans: 116

Doris Evans: 53 (bottom)

Patricia Evans: 41, 71

Gregory Fox: 3, 5, 10, 11, 22, 23, 25, 26, 30, 38, 39 (center & bottom), 49, 60, 61 (bottom), 62, 66, 72, 75 (top right), 79, 86, 88 (bottom), 89 (bottom), 92, 93, 96, 97, 100, 102

High/Scope Demonstration Preschool staff: 12, 14 (bottom right), 52

Tricia Kruse: 53 (center)

Library of Congress Cataloging-in-Publication Data
Evans, Betsy.
  "I know what's next!" : preschool transitions without tears or turmoil
: the teacher's idea book series / Betsy Evans.
      p. cm.
  Includes bibliographical references and index.
  ISBN 978-1-57379-297-4 (soft cover : alk. paper) 1. Education,
Preschool. 2. Early childhood education. I. Title.

  LB1140.2.E87 2007
  372.21--dc22

2006037768

Printed in the United States of America
10 9 8 7 6 5 4 3

For Zoe Reeves Evans and all the small children who are counting on us to let them know what is coming next.

Contents

Acknowledgments

Transitions are a lifelong challenge for both adults and children; we all need strategies and support to negotiate transitions successfully. I would like to thank the staff of the High/Scope Foundation for their support during my transition from teacher to teacher-trainer and author. These last 18 years spent in collaboration with foundation staff have been a rich and rewarding journey that has fostered my understanding of active learning and the wants and needs of young children, and helped me to find effective ways to communicate this knowledge to adults. In particular, the inspired work of the late David Weikart and of Mary Hohmann, described with such clarity in *Educating Young Children: Active Learning Practices for Preschool and Child Care Programs* (Hohmann & Weikart, 2002), has been a philosophical and practical foundation for all of us in the field of early childhood education. The thoughtful guidance of Ruth Strubank, my TOT (Training of Trainers) Program trainer, helped me to develop the awareness and courage I needed to stand up before others and clearly articulate myself. And the expert feedback of my editor, Nancy Brickman, continues to support my growth as an author.

I would also like to acknowledge the contributions of the many teachers whom I have been fortunate to meet and observe throughout my time as a trainer. Teachers from Bloomingdale Head Start, Columbia University Head Start, and Union Settlement Association Child Care Centers in New York City; ACE Integration Head Start, Brooklyn, New York; High/Scope Demonstration Preschool in Ypsilanti, Michigan; Joyce Carey Head Start Center in Newburgh, New York; Giving Tree School in Gill, Massachusetts; Little Sprouts Child Enrichment Centers in Andover, Massachusetts; and Montachusett Regional YMCA Preschool, Burbank Child Development Center, and Montachusett Opportunity Council Head Start in Fitchburg, Massachusetts, contributed many ideas and strategies for this book. Ideas and support also came from my colleagues, Julie Austin and Sarah Pirtle, who contributed musical ideas and large-group-time suggestions, and Rachael Underwood, who as always inspires me to keep feelings and playfulness at the forefront as I work with teachers and children.

A special thanks goes to Heather Sky Fulton, who, with her artistic talents, created the illustrations in this book. She was able to bring life and creativity to the sketches and dialogue I gave her, illuminating real people — their feelings and perspectives — with humor and clarity.

And finally, thanks go to the newest member of my family, my first grandchild, exuberant and sensitive Zoe, as well as three other young members of my world family, Stan, Kate, and Ella. These little ones help me continuously reflect on the varied nature of transitions as I participate in the very real and challenging changes in their everyday lives. In the end, it is always the children who teach us.

1
Introduction —
Keys to Successful Transitions

Children who attend preschool and child care programs experience frequent transitions of all kinds — arriving and departing to and from the child care setting, separating from parents, moving from one activity to another throughout the day, and sometimes, shifting to another classroom or caregiver before rejoining their parents. Eventually, they must make the biggest transition of all — departure to kindergarten or a new program.

These changes pose many challenges, both cognitive and emotional, for young children. Children may not understand what to do next, where to go, or why they have to stop what they are doing, and their confusion and frustration can lead to behavior upsets. These challenging situations, however, can also be learning opportunities. Teachers and caregivers can prevent problems, reduce conflict, and encourage learning by planning for the obvious transitions that are predictable in a child's day, as well as for those that are unexpected. If adults can invest the time and energy needed to support children during these times, they can minimize disruptions and wasted time. At the same time, they can help children build the skills they will need to cope with the wide variety of transitions they will encounter throughout their lives.

A transition is a time when children experience a change in activities, places, or people. While this definition is simple, the realities of transitions for young children are much more complex. To understand the challenges transitions pose for preschoolers, it can help to consider all the transitions we as adults typically have to make during a workday. These

Transition routines, sometimes as simple as a wave at the door, foster the ability to walk through that door confidently thinking, "I know what's next!"

might include numerous conversational transitions from one topic or person to another, frequent work transitions from one type of task to another, as well as the more complex emotional transitions of separating from loved ones in the morning, sitting blank-faced in a commuter train or car, and finally arriving at a fast-paced workplace where thoughts and emotions must remain in balance. With the end of the day comes another series of shifts as we try to shed the stresses of work and reconnect with family members.

If we think about the demands such changes place on us — adults who are accustomed to the shifting requirements of each part of the day — it is easier to grasp the impact of this on children and the importance of planning for the many transitions that they must make. As we plan, it's important to consider ways to meet our own adult needs as children change activities. We also need to think about the characteristics of each kind of transition, as well as children's differing responses to changes in activities and caregivers.

Some children manage easily during transitions while others do not, and the transitions themselves may be lengthy or quick, complicated or simple. Consider, for example, the many different kinds of transitions young children who attend preschool experience in a typical day. The day begins with children leaving home and all that is familiar and coming to the early childhood setting, and this may include an hour or more spent at a baby sitter's home in between. Once they arrive, they contend with rapid shifts in people, places, and activities as they enter the building, put away their belongings, wash their hands, eat breakfast, brush their teeth and use the toilet, and in some programs, begin the routine in one classroom and then move to another. They then participate in all the other transitions associated with the program's educational routine, for example, going from individual choice time, to a small-group activity, to story time, to outdoor play, and so forth. As children move through the day, they also experience planned or unexpected changes in their companions — the presence of a new caregiving adult and/or the absence of a favorite classmate.

In addition to the transitions associated with the child care setting, children may also be affected emotionally during the day by family changes that are ongoing: a new baby, the death of a pet, a household move, longer parental work hours, a divorce. These types of family transitions can make some children feel unbalanced, as if they are walking on Jell-O. Even during the simplest of daily activities, they may feel unsteady and unsure. Highly sensitized to change, they feel emotionally unsettled because they are constantly on the lookout for the next transition.

Since there are so many differences in the factors affecting children, no single approach to transitions will work with every child. Some children manage numerous transitions and appear unruffled, while others need calm, prepared adults and very predictable schedules and routines to help them feel safe.

Key Principles for Supporting Children During Transitions

While every situation is different, the following key principles, when used consistently, will help adults guide children successfully through a wide variety of transitions.

✔ *Take the child's perspective, keeping the developmental characteristics of preschoolers in mind.*

During transitions, teachers are often busy attending to routine tasks while also guiding children through the shift in activities, so it can be difficult to consider the child's perspective. Yet it is important to remember that children's attentions are also divided — they are busy interacting with other children as they move from space to space or between activities and are easily distracted by the materi-

Getting down to the child's level helps adults maintain their focus on the child's perspective.

als or by the actions of others. Moreover, children at this level of development are usually able to keep only one or two things in mind at a time, so they can easily become unfocused and forget what they are supposed to do next. Thus, it is essential to be patient and willing to consider children's needs along with your own.

Some additional developmental characteristics to remember at these times are that young children are egocentric (self-centered), physically expressive, and still learning language and social skills. As a result, they often do not see the "big picture" of what needs to happen next and may physically express their frustration or verbalize their feelings in a hurtful

Children are better prepared for upcoming changes if they can literally see them coming and are included in the preparations. Here children watch a new floor being installed in their school.

way. When this happens, be prepared to take a problem-solving approach. Usually this means encouraging children to discuss the problem, but during a transition there may not be time to talk things over. In this case, gently and clearly give children limited choices and acknowledge their feelings, while patiently moving forward with the transition: "You've had a lot of fun outside and are feeling frustrated that we need to go in for lunch." (Pause, giving the child time to see that you really do understand.) "We do need to go in for lunch. Shall we hold hands and skip, or hop like bunnies to the door?" (For more on the use of problem solving during transitions, see pp. 61 and 71. For details on the problem-solving process, see *You Can't Come to My Birthday Party! Conflict Resolution With Young Children,* Evans, 2002.)

To understand the child's perspective, it is also helpful to remember that children's ability to grasp concepts of time is very different from adults'. Children are interested in the "here and now"; their experience of time is not based on watching the clock but on physical activities and obvious changes that remind them of events like meals and group times. For example, putting on their coats signals outside time, and table-setting signals the approach of a meal time. Adults can best help children predict the beginning of a transition by not depending too heavily on conventional time units, and by not referring to time units at all if the transition is more than ten minutes away. Very young children understand their world through concrete visual cues that show what will happen next; the verbal reminders that work for an eight-year-old will not work as well with preschoolers. Therefore, for this age group, it is best to signal transitions by using pictures, large salt timers, or simple rituals, like playing a special piece of music.

✔ *As you plan what to do during shifts in activities, consider what distractions or additional tasks you will have.*

If tables must be cleaned off as children move from table activities to hand washing, if cots must be laid out as children arrive from outside, or if parents are trying to talk to you as you help children brush their teeth after breakfast, it will be difficult to give children the support they need. If there are tasks to be done during transitions, make a clear plan for

This child points out where she wants to play on a planning chart, a visual aid that allows her to "see" the transition from planning to choice time.

who will do what. Ideally, there will be one adult for the task and at least one to support the children. If this is not possible, using a well-known song or a familiar activity (plan this beforehand) may help children manage the transition more independently.

✔ *For each shift in activities, make a plan that includes an activity with choices, a warning, and extra time for the transition.*

Success during transitions is all about predictability and a sense of control, with a good dash of fun included. Before the transition occurs, consider the children's concerns and needs, and be prepared to explain thoroughly what will happen. Think of something enjoyable to do during the transition and consider ways to give children choices. Just before, give a warning with the number of minutes until the change, perhaps asking children to help with the warnings and the signal, thus increasing their sense of control.

✔ *Give children the time they need to move through transitions playfully and to express any feelings they have.*

Taking time to acknowledge a child's feelings about separation will make the rest of the day go more smoothly.

As the transition begins, be ready to acknowledge children's feelings. Children may be excited about, or resistant, to the change — give all such emotions time for full expression, rather than trying to suppress or stop them. While adults often worry that this will slow things down, allowing children to express their reactions will generally make it easier for children to move more smoothly from one activity to the next. It is always best to take an unhurried approach to transitions, moving through the transition both playfully and slowly so that children enjoy the process and have time to develop the skills to negotiate all transitions successfully.

About This Book

In the rest of this book, we explore the principles discussed here in depth. We challenge the notion that transition times are fleeting and inherently empty of learning opportunities. We offer many suggestions, ideas, and strategies for managing the challenges transitions present for children, teachers, and parents.

The illustrations in each chapter highlight specific problems that often occur during transitions. These "picture-stories" are intended to help you envision the experience from both adult and child perspectives. In each pair of drawings a frequently used approach is shown first, followed by an illustration of an alternative strategy. The first scene shows an adult who has a useful intention, though his or her initial approach may be ineffective. When the same adult responds with a different strategy in the second illustration, it is clear that sometimes all the adult needs is a slightly different perspective to give the support and understanding children require.

Each chapter also includes a list of "Top Tips." This is a quick summary of key points for responding to the challenges discussed in depth in the chapter.

Chapter 2 explores the process of orienting children new to the program, strategies and routines for daily arrivals and departures, as well as the emotional challenges presented by separations from parents. This chapter also offers ideas for easing the transition from one classroom to another or one preschool program to another, and from preschool to kindergarten programs. Special consideration is also given to strategies for supporting parents at these times.

Chapter 3 presents suggestions and ideas for supporting children as they make transitions from one part of the daily routine to another (for example from an indoor choice time to outdoor time). Teachers often expect such shifts to go smoothly, without special planning. But children, with their less developed sense of time, need concrete reminders of what is going to happen next and other support to move through these potentially chaotic parts of the day.

In Chapter 4, the self-care requirements that involve movement from one space to another (for example from classroom to bathroom) or turn-taking (such as for hand washing, toothbrushing, or toileting) will be considered. Planning for these experiences involves considering ways to keep the group safe while engaging them in activities. For adults, these times are often busy and full of distractions, while for children these can be empty waiting times. New ideas that replace the tradition of lining-up for self-care tasks are presented; "circling-up" is described as an engaging and educational alternative.

Chapter 5 explores the concept, premise, and challenge of cleanup time. First, the tradition of regarding cleanup as primarily a transition period will be reconsidered. When viewed only as a transition, cleanup is usually everyone's least favorite time of the day because the focus is on stopping play and on carrying out the tiresome chores of cleaning. But

Principles for Successful Transitions

- Take the child's perspective, keeping the developmental characteristics of preschoolers in mind.

- Consider what distractions or additional tasks you will have.

- For each shift in activities, make a plan that includes an activity with choices, a warning, and extra time for the transition.

- Take an unhurried approach to transitions, moving through the transition both playfully and slowly. Be ready to acknowledge children's feelings, and be prepared to take a problem-solving approach if problems arise.

when this necessary experience is also seen as a full-fledged daily routine component that can meet learning objectives and actually be *enjoyed* by children and adults, the experience is transformed. Play can continue in the form of lively cleanup activities. Many ideas for restructuring and having fun during cleanup time are discussed in this chapter.

The appendix presents reproducible materials that can be used to educate parents as they support their children during key transitions. Included are a letter to parents to request a home visit before their child enters the program, a letter and handout about separation anxiety, a handout about daily departures, and a handout about moving on to kindergarten.

• ⌐

The underlying premise of this book is that the time spent in transitions does not have to be wasted time for children. Children often move through transitions feeling confused, unsupported, and sometimes unsafe, and this can result in upsets or conflicts. Or, they may spend the time between activities feeling bored and looking for ways to be active, often to the dismay and disapproval of teachers. If adults can rethink these empty transition times, they can transform them into learning experiences that are as full and rich as other parts of the day. Both children and their caregivers then benefit from the predictability and the increased stability of a classroom in which everyone moves calmly through the day and the year, negotiating changes with grace, fun, and a healthy sense of how to function creatively and cooperatively as a community.

2

Letting Go and Moving On — Orientation, Arrivals and Departures, Room-to-Room and Kindergarten Transitions

This chapter explores some of the most challenging transitions for young children and the adults in their lives — the transitions from home to the child care setting and from one child care setting to another, including daily arrivals and departures to and from the program, the adjustment to a new classroom or new program, and finally, the transition from the preschool to the kindergarten. The chapter presents supportive interaction strategies and specific activities that can facilitate successful transitions at these times, highlighting the child's perspective throughout the discussion. Special attention is given to supporting children's healthy expression of emotion as they negotiate these challenging experiences, because these particular transitions so often bring strong emotional reactions from children.

Orientation of children new to a program and daily arrivals and departures both require special planning. The sections that follow explore preparations, activities, routines, and adult-child interaction strategies that can sustain children's emotional balance and well-being during these times, making these transitions go more smoothly for both children and adults.

Orientation: Preparing Children for a New Setting

Orientation guidelines
Keep the following general guidelines in mind as you think about ways to prepare children to enter the program.

✔ *Understand the connection between children's feelings and the need to visualize the new setting in concrete ways.*

As children anticipate entering a new preschool program, they often have strong emotional reactions: excitement, anxiety, fear, anger, sadness, or a combination of these feelings. Young children's feelings about an upcoming change to a new setting are often particularly intense because they have difficulty imagining the new setting. Though adults often attempt to prepare children by telling them about the new place, this information is often too abstract to be meaningful to children. Until they visit the new program or become acquainted with some of their new caregivers and playmates (activities suggested in the next section), they are unable to think clearly about the transition. Since they lack a concrete physical context for a discussion of the future, much of their reaction is likely to be emotional. Though their questions are often about the physical details ("Where is the school?" "Will you be there?" "Will my friends be there?" "What does the teacher look like?" "Will there be a guinea pig?"), the underlying questions, which are harder for them to ask directly, are emotional ("Am I going to be safe?" "Is it going to feel okay to me?" "Will people be nice to me there?"). For these reasons, many of the suggestions presented in the sections that follow address ways both to give children concrete information about the new setting and to encourage young children to express their emotions fully, so that they can move on to make the adjustments necessary for a smooth transition.

Children who have had the opportunity to learn about the new people and activities in their school are more likely to come to school happy and eager to start the day.

✔ *Prepare in advance for children's first day.*

By making preparations in advance for children's arrival to a new setting, you will ensure that children's first day goes as smoothly as possible. Your preparations might include planning special orientation events and activities, as well as considering how to give children the emotional support that is essential as they adjust to the separation from loved ones and to the beginning of new friendships. Following are some activities and strategies to use with children entering the program.

Orientation activities and strategies

Home visits. Children will need to make many new adjustments as they enter a program, so it can be very helpful if the adjustment process can begin in familiar surroundings — the child's own home or perhaps the home of a relative who cares for the child during the day. Home visits allow children to get to know their new teachers or caregivers in a safe and comfortable setting. During the home visit, children may enjoy showing the visiting adult or adults their room, a favorite toy or pet, or a backyard swing. Classroom adults can talk with the child about this shared experience when the child arrives at school, and such conversations help to strengthen the "bridge" between home and school. The home visit also gives parents a chance to ask questions, which facilitates their own transition to the program. During the home visit, teachers sometimes share written information with parents about ways that they can become involved in their child's program. Teachers may also ask children to choose a letter link or other personal symbol (see p. 12) or a special picture that will appear together with their name on their cubby on the first day. Families might be asked for a family photo to include in the cubby. All of these home visit activities will help to build trust between the program adults and children and their families, easing tension and uncertainty.

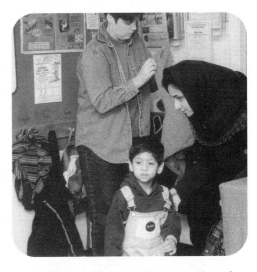

Open houses allow children to explore the new setting while supported by their family members.

Open house. Scheduling a time for children to visit the program with family, relatives, and/or neighbors creates an opportunity for children to get to know the physical space of their new classroom while supported by the significant adults in their life. The open house is an informal drop-in time, lasting a couple of hours, with time for meeting other families and perhaps for a large-group time of singing and/or reading a story together. Children might meet the classroom pet, see their chosen symbol on their cubby, or get acquainted with a new friend. Program adults focus their attention on supporting the children's exploration of the space, avoiding formal presentations and paperwork. The emphasis is on children gaining a sense that the new setting is a safe, fun place to be — a place they will now look forward to exploring on their own.

Short beginning days. Scheduling one or two very brief program days can ensure that children are not overwhelmed by the length of a typical day. Children arrive at a specified time and stay for only one or two hours. If there are two short days, a parent may stay with his or her child on the first day, if necessary. Depending on the child's readiness, the parent may choose to stay or not to stay on the second day. Often, short days are arranged so that a smaller than normal group of children are present. One or two of the daily routine components can be introduced at this time, with adults remaining flexible as they observe how each child reacts to the setting and activities. Though somewhat complicated to implement, these short sessions make a successful transition to the program much more likely, offsetting possible inconveniences to parents and teachers.

Creation of individual spaces. Preparing a cubby space or other container for individual children's possessions gives children a sense of belonging. As discussed earlier, the space can be personalized by posting the child's name, letter link or symbol, and perhaps a family photo. Family photo displays and/or photo attendance boards that allow children to "sign in" can also be prepared in advance of the child's arrival. All of these visual signs let children know that they are part of this new community, helping to reduce any feelings of uneasiness.

Letter Links and Personal Symbols

Giving each child a unique "personal symbol" (such as a heart for Mary, a truck for Jack) to identify with and to use as a label next to his or her name (on cubbies, sign-in lists, helper charts, etc.) is a strategy that has been used for years in diverse preschool settings. Children who come to preschool not yet able to recognize their own name can very quickly recognize their own symbol, especially if they have chosen it themselves. Even for children who know their own name, it is much easier to recognize (and read) their classmates' names — wherever they are displayed — when each name is accompanied by a symbol they have come to associate with that person. (This is especially

helpful when two or more children have the same first name.) Pictorial symbols are more concrete, more distinguishable, and therefore easier for young children to remember and read than the letter symbols that make up our written language.

A relatively new way of using personal symbols is to link children's symbols to the letter and sound of their first name (Hohmann & DeBruin-Parecki, 2003). Rather than randomly chosen symbols, each child is given an image or "letter link" for a word that begins with the same letter and sound as his or her first name. So Max might have a motorcycle

for his letter link, Lindsay a leaf, and Shawn a shoe. Whenever possible, the child's pictorial image is always shown with the first letter of the name and used with the child's nametag. This strategy can help children begin to understand the alphabetic principle — that the sounds in spoken words are linked to the letters in written words — in a very functional way.

— From *Preschool Readers and Writers: Early Literacy Strategies for Teachers* (pp. 123, 125), by Linda Weikel Ranweiler, 2004, Ypsilanti, MI: High/Scope Press.

Arrivals (Drop-Off Time)

It's important to plan carefully for children's daily arrivals; otherwise, children can be overwhelmed by the emotional demands of separating from loved ones and/or the practical demands of carrying out the many small tasks that must be accomplished at this time. Following are some guidelines.

Guidelines for arrival time

✔ *Consider the developmental characteristics that affect children at drop-off time.*

In considering how to plan for children's arrivals, it can be very helpful to keep in mind certain developmental characteristics that make the home-to-school transition challenging for young children. First, young children's *sense of time* is concrete. Children's thinking is tied to physical events and characteristics, rather than the clock, so it is hard for them to understand the adult's urgent but abstract need to be on time. It is helpful to ask parents to allow extra time for drop-off during the first few days. *One-thing-at-a-time thinking* is another developmental trait that affects children during home-to-school transitions. At this stage young children can focus on just one or two tasks or people at once. Since the start of the day's session often involves many tasks and/or people, this time is particularly challenging for young children. Preschoolers are also developing the *physical dexterity* needed to manage their clothing and possessions independently. Since these self-care skills are just emerging, getting clothing on or off and gathering possessions can be time consuming.

Seeing that a personal space is ready for their belongings helps children feel comfortable entering school. Children's spaces are labeled with their names and letter links or personal symbols (left) and may also include a family photo as shown in the top photo.

Therefore, it is also important to make sure that children have adequate warnings, plenty of support, and plenty of time to carry out the necessary activities. Note that these same developmental characteristics also affect children as they reconnect with their parents at the end of the day.

✔ *To ensure children's security and independence, establish a consistent arrival routine.*

The routine will vary depending on whether children arrive by bus or with parents, whether everyone arrives at the same time, whether early and/or late arrivals are a standard part of the program, whether breakfast is served, and so forth. The routine may include putting away personal belongings, putting a photo card on an attendance board, signing in, and preparing for breakfast or message board time. (These and other possible arrival activities are described in more detail in the section that begins on p. 20.) In addition to your general arrival routine, each child may have an individual arrival routine developed in conjunction with his or her parents. (Such routines are described in greater detail on p. 17 and in the parent handout given in the appendix.)

Top: Using the sign-in board, this child thinks carefully about the letters in her name.

Above: After signing in, this child looks for his name and places his star on a board.

✔ **Be prepared to support children individually as they arrive.**

It is essential for teachers and caregivers to consider each child's individual needs upon arrival. This is one of the most challenging times of the day, as children may be sleepy, hungry, or reluctant to participate. There are a wide variety of experiences that can happen for children as they arrive, depending on their personal needs and the program's schedule.

The time taken to support individual children as they arrive can make a difference that will last all day. Some children need one-on-one time with an adult, some need time alone, and others are happy to jump right into play with materials or other children. Inviting children to join a gathering or a breakfast group is important, as long as it is clear that it is the child's choice whether or not to join. Arrival rituals are most useful if they are flexible. Observing how a child enters and facilitating what works best for him or her can help the whole day get off to a smooth start. Each child needs to enter the setting at his or her own pace.

✔ **Greet children individually.**

Regardless of the details of a program's arrival routine, a very important part for children is the initial greeting by one of the teachers or caregivers in the program. This sets the tone for the day and lets children know they are truly valued and wanted as part of the group. As children come into the building, from the bus or with a family member, one caregiver should be completely available to greet them. Depending on the number of children arriving, there may need to be more than one adult available for this important part of the day.

Observe closely to see what type of greeting works best for each child. Some children enjoy big, boisterous greetings, hugs, and noisy chatter. Other children find this overwhelming and show a preference for a quieter, less physical approach. Be sensitive to the body language cues of individual children as to what sort of greeting they enjoy most. Try to keep the focus of the greeting on the child, rather than on other factors, such as clothing. "You look really excited to be here this morning!" is more child focused than "What a pretty dress you have on today!" By taking a few min-

Be sensitive to children's individual needs for support as they arrive.

utes to listen to children's stories or to hear about a new baby or other important event, you can help children connect with you more quickly, easing the way for them to join the community for the day.

✔ *Be prepared for separation difficulties.*

(The information in this section is directed at teachers and caregivers, but it is essential for parents as well. It may be discussed with parents at a meeting or home visit, or in a handout. A sample handout for parents is given in the appendix.)

Most children arrive at preschool or child care looking forward excitedly to the day. However, it is not unusual for some children to become anxious and possibly quite upset as they get off the bus or separate from the adults who have brought them to the child care setting. It is essential to be prepared for a range of reactions, as the intensity of the experience varies from child to child. Fully supporting one or two upset children can help to avoid the "domino effect" of crying children upsetting other children nearby.

As you support children at these times, it can be reassuring to keep in mind that separation anxiety is a normal and healthy aspect of development for children who are becoming independent; yet however normal, it still requires an accepting and supportive response from adults. Children's distress indicates they are beginning to develop a sense of themselves as separate from their parents or significant caregivers. Understandably, the prospect of independence and autonomy may be frightening to children.

The intensity and timing of separation anxiety will vary from child to child. It may appear when children first enter the program, or later on when they are familiar with it. It may be triggered not only by the departures of family members at the beginning of the day but also by changes in the program, such as new staff, or by family changes, such as a new baby or a move. Sometimes there is no clear explanation for the sudden appearance of separation anxiety. The important point to remember is that children are experiencing emotional distress and need the support of an understanding adult; however, this distress does *not* mean that the child should necessarily leave the program.

Though taking steps toward independence is a normal part of children's development at this age, it is useful to remember that not all children are enthusiastic about becoming independent. Some children will be very excited about entering the program and will make the transition easily. Others may be hesitant; still others may become hysterical. Teachers, caregivers, and parents need to discuss beforehand what they will do if a child does become very upset, and in preparation, develop consistent and responsive strategies for reassuring the child. As the school year unfolds, teachers and caregivers need to discuss (out of the child's earshot) whether the child is progressing toward adjustment and how continued reassurance can be given. With support and time, most children do adjust.

✔ **Acknowledge children's feelings as needed.**

As illustrated by the drawings on pages 18 and 19, a child experiencing separation difficulties needs adults to respond with warm support. This means voicing understanding and acceptance of the child's sad or angry feelings and perhaps offering physical reassurance with a hand on the shoulder or a hug. Parents can help a distressed child by simply saying, perhaps several times, "I can see that you're feeling really sad that I'm leaving. I know this is hard." A statement like this lets the child know that even though Mom has to leave, she understands his or her confusing emotions. Similarly, it can be helpful if caregivers say something like "It looks like you're feeling really mad [or sad] that your dad has left."

Sometimes adults try to stop the expression of children's feelings with comments like "Be a big boy" or "It's okay," or deceptions like "She'll be right back." These tactics are not recommended. It's also more supportive for adults to avoid long explanations of what the parent will be doing; such explanations are not reassuring, as the child is focused on his or her experience *right now*. Distraction is another often-used (but not recommended) strategy. The adult, with the good intention of making the child feel better, suggests an activity or toy. This may appear to work temporarily; however, the feelings are only submerged and may resurface again, cued by something as simple as the word *mommy*. Once a child's feelings have been acknowledged and he or she has calmed, *then* the adult might suggest activities.

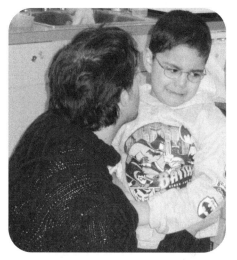

When a child becomes upset during transitions, reassurance is most effective when given by a patient adult who gets on the child's level and calmly accepts and names the child's feelings. Note that the child is looking away from the adult, as is typical for preschoolers. Adults should never force a child to make eye contact.

Program staff (and parents) can best help children during separations by simply describing the feelings that they have observed them expressing, as in the examples given. When such statements are made in a heartfelt manner, children are deeply reassured that the adults at the center understand how very difficult the separation is for them. When children experience the support of caregivers who are willing to listen to and understand their strongest emotions, the child develops trust, security, and attachment to the classroom adults. As children calm, adults may be able to problem-solve with them, letting them know when they will be picked up and what activities they might choose to start their day: "Zakera, you were feeling really sad, and now you look ready to play. Let's look at our daily routine and see when your dad will pick you up, and then you can choose where you'd like to play."

Here are a few things to keep in mind as you acknowledge children's feelings. Name the child's feelings with a soothing tone, and look for signs that the child is calming. The reassurance that this response gives may not always be immediately apparent; in fact the child may cry even more intensely now that you have given "permission" for fully expressing feelings. Avoid telling the child to "calm down"; instead you may need to repeat your acknowledgment over and over until the child's crying slows and his or her body relaxes.

Children benefit from such acknowledgments in many ways: they get to know adults as accepting, understanding people; they learn that strong feelings are a healthy part of life; and they learn how to express those feelings constructively. Once their feelings are fully expressed, they are able to regain emotional balance and will be much more effective learners as a result. According to Jane Healy's *Your Child's Growing Mind* (1994), strong emotions can interfere with learning because the part of the brain that processes emotions is directly connected to the brain's thinking functions. "The emotional brain…[is] an integral part of the circuitry that activates and directs messages to the cortex, and the crux of the attention system. It can either facilitate learning or, quite literally, shut down the thinking systems" (p. 24).

✔ *Prepare parents for children's reactions.*

Teachers and caregivers can help parents prepare for the reactions children may have when they are dropped off. Many parents may be surprised by the intensity of their child's outburst. Unsure of the best way to respond, they may scold or shame the child. Discussing with parents what to expect and how they might respond can help everyone cope more effectively.

It is helpful to counsel parents that smooth transitions begin at home. Avoiding upsets at the very beginning of the day helps to ease the transition to school. Suggest that parents try using a salt timer at home with their child in the morning to warn them that it is almost time to leave. (As discussed earlier, salt timers can help to make time concrete and visible for young children.) As parents tell the child "Five more minutes until we leave for school [or child care]," they can turn over the salt timer so that the child will be able to "see" time passing.

Encourage parents who are dropping off their child to participate in a "separation plan" that might include at least some of these arrival rituals: putting a photo on a board, settling the child in at the breakfast table, or joining the group as children read the message board. It can be fun and reassuring for a child to have a parent take part in these first activities of the day; the child also benefits from knowing the parent is interested in his or her activities at school. Encourage parents to decide which activities they will stay for and to stick to this routine consistently. If parents have made a separation plan and informed the classroom adults about it, it will be clear to everyone when they will actually say goodbye and the separation will be easier.

At the end of this book are some reproducible materials you can use as you orient new children and educate parents about home-to-school transitions (see the appendix). Included are a letter requesting a home visit before the child starts school, and a parent handout and accompanying letter on separation anxiety.

✔ *As you discuss separation difficulties with parents, it is also important to consider their needs at these times.*

It can be painful and scary for parents to leave a child who is upset and challenging for caregivers to respond to the parents' distress. If parents

Instead of ignoring or trying to stop emotional outbursts, sending a message that these feelings are bad or bothersome…

...name and fully accept the child's sad or angry feelings, letting him or her know that you understand how hard the separation is for them.

and teachers can openly listen to each other's concerns, this will help the child, parent, and program adults make a smoother adjustment. If a child is very upset at a parent's departure, the parent and teacher can arrange to talk by phone after an hour or two. Discourage having the parent speak to the child; this may re-trigger upset feelings.

Arrival routines and activities

Following are some ideas for beginning the program day with children. Each program must decide which routines will work best for its group of children and program structure, but some elements are common to all. In all programs children will enter and put their clothing and belongings away in their individual spaces. Taking attendance in some form (photo boards, name pockets, sign-in books, and so forth) is another universal part of the routine. Included in this section are ideas for structuring this so children take an active part in recording their arrivals. After attendance-taking, the next part of day may be breakfast, followed by tooth-brushing; for others, the day may begin with a large-group meeting (called "greeting time" in many programs). Beginning the day by gathering with the entire group helps children reconnect with their school community for the day. This is an opportunity to greet classmates and briefly preview the day's activities. Such greeting times are most effective for preschoolers when they are active for everyone and last no more than 10–15 minutes. See the next section for ideas for leading into and conducting this whole-group activity. More ideas for large-group meetings are given in Chapter 3.

As you consider arrival routines for your group, assess children's developmental needs as well as their individual interests. The following activity ideas are for children at varying developmental levels. Some ideas are for children to complete individually, some work well with a large group, and some may be used either way. For instance, the photo board is the simplest developmentally of the ways to record attendance. The sign-in board is more challenging. The attendance games are designed for large-group gatherings, and the message board can be used by individuals as they arrive or by a large group that gathers and informally "reads" the messages together. A combination of activities that are well suited to your group of children and are repeated every day will add to the consistency of the day's start, giving the children predictability and security.

Cubbies. Children stow their belongings in the cubby space you have prepared. Make sure that there is adequate space for children's clothing, for personal items, such as children's security object or a toy from home, and for things children create during the day.

Photo boards. Make children's photos available in a container or on a table. Each photo can be labeled with the child's name and letter link (or symbol), laminated, and backed with Velcro. As they arrive, children find their photo and post it on a board before moving to the next part of the routine.

Name pocket. This is an alternative to the photo board. Children use an attendance board consisting of rows of cloth pockets. Cards with each child's letter link or personal symbol and name are available in a basket or box. As they arrive, children find their card and put it in a pocket. Sometimes the name pockets are also used for "helper choices" (see p. 60), with helper job cards placed in the pockets at a later time.

Sign-in boards. Children use a special sign-in space as they arrive. This might be a dry-erase board, a chalkboard, or a book where they can draw their letter-linked picture or symbol or write their name in real letters, letterlike forms, drawings, or scribbles. It is important for adults to accept all forms of developing writing as children sign in and to provide writing help if requested. Post a list of children's names and their letter links or symbols for them to refer to as they sign in.

One-area-open activity time. Some programs find it helpful as children are arriving to have one or two areas open, one of which will eventually be used for the first whole-group meeting of the day. These areas may be spaces that have books, puzzles, or manipulatives that can be put away quickly. Children can use these materials informally until everyone has gathered. Post "closed" signs by the other areas, such as the symbol for the area with a circle with a line through it, to visually remind children that these areas are not yet open for play.

Greeting time. At greeting time, one adult is posted near the door to greet children while the other adult stays in a designated area of the classroom to work with children as they come in. Easily-put-away materials, such as books or puzzles, are available for children to play with and explore informally. Parents may join in by reading a story or playing with their child for a few minutes before leaving. Once everyone has arrived, greeting time may become a more formal time in which the whole group looks at a message board or engages in games, songs, or a story. A 10- to 15-minute large-group meeting is developmentally appropriate, as long as the activities include active learning for everyone.

Attendance games. When everyone has gathered in a large group, one option is to play alliteration or rhyming games with children's names that stimulate participation from everyone. For example, "I spy with my little eye someone whose name rhymes with *bam*." (The children respond, "Sam!") Or, "I'm thinking of someone whose name starts like /s/ — *snake.*" ("Sam!") Sam's name can then be checked off on a posted list where everyone can see the letters of his name.

Reading messages. "Reading" a classroom message board with information about the day's activities is another common arrival activity for individual children or the whole group. For details, see "The Message Board" (p. 24).

Calendar activities. If calendar and/or weather prediction activities are required by state standards, be sure these are carried out in developmentally appropriate ways, using symbols and patterns that children can understand. Preschool children's developing understanding of time is focused primarily on "yesterday" and "today" (concepts that have a con-

One Program's Arrival Routine

In this carefully planned sequence of opening activities, one activity flows smoothly into the next, needless transitions are eliminated, waiting times are active, and children's independence in following the routine is encouraged throughout. Family members often join in the first few activities of the day.

1. Children are greeted at the door by one teacher.

2. Children take off their coats and hang them on hooks labeled with their name and letter link.

3. A child signs in using his own form of writing.

4. As students are greeted at the door, the other children explore books alone...

5. or read with another teacher...

6. or read with a family member.

7. After a teacher signals the end of book-reading with a song, "It's time to put the books away," some of the children begin putting the books away while others finish up their stories. Teachers signal the next activity by singing, "Put your bottom on the floor and read the message board" (see p. 24).

(see p. 24)

8. Message board time starts in the same area, eliminating a transition. Some parents are still present as the group reads the messages together. The messages, told in pictures and words, let children know there is a visitor with a camera today and that there are new materials in the art area.

9. Still gathered in the same place, the group transitions to large-group time. It is one child's turn to pick the first song, and the group pats their knees and chants "I wonder what he'll pick" as they wait for the child to choose the song.

10. Large-group comes to an end with an active song. (Some parents are still present.)

11. The teacher asks everybody to freeze in place.

12. The teacher "unfreezes" each child with a tap on the head and one by one, the children go to their planning table.

The Message Board

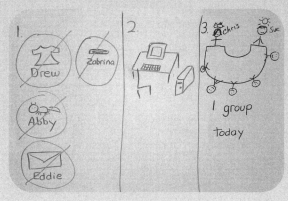

This board tells children which children are absent, alerts them to a new program in the computer area, and lets them know there will be only one small group that day.

Reading the message board with the class is a very effective way to bring the preschool community together at the beginning of the day's session, as well as a rich learning opportunity. The goal is to engage children in the process of decoding the messages, an emergent reading experience that helps them transition into the activities of the day.

"Write" your messages (using pictures, symbols, and words) on a dry-erase board, a chalkboard, or a large piece of paper. Typical messages describe which children and adults are absent that day; new materials available in particular areas; and changes in the daily routine, such as a field trip or special visitor. Children "read" and guess the messages either on their own or with the group.

The message board may be prepared by classroom adults before children arrive, or by an adult and a group of children who have just arrived. Besides drawings, photos, and symbols, the message board should also have some numbers, letters, and words. The emphasis, however, is on the pictures and symbols; since all children are "picture readers," all can succeed at "reading" the board. A pattern for the week of home and school days can be included as a "calendar"; teachers can write the name of the weekday on it.

Some teachers are hesitant to create a message board because they feel they cannot draw well enough. Even very simple drawings

can be easily understood by children, however — stick figures are fine. Messages may sometimes even include real objects, for example, a lost mitten, or a sample of a new material available in the classroom!

Interpreting messages together can be a very enjoyable, informal group activity, with lots of conversation as children try to read and guess the messages. Each child interacts with the messages in his or her own way, with some children recognizing familiar words, letters, or numbers and others using the pictures or symbols as they read or guess the messages. Sometimes parents may join in with this part of the arrival routine.

The message board is kept out throughout the daily routine so that children can refer to it when they wish, reminding themselves of what will happen next, new materials available, or which classmates are not in school that day. Children arriving late can read the messages (helped by their friends, if necessary), allowing them to catch up on the news of the day.

As children decode the messages on the board, they are practicing the concept that pictures, objects, and words can be used to stand for real objects, events, and people. The message board is a reading experience that meets a practical need for information, so children are also learning about the functions of reading. Teachers and caregivers who use message boards find that children not only look forward to receiving information in this way, taking pride in their ability to read the messages, but also seem to remember the information more easily when it is given in this form. The challenge of decoding symbols, pictures, and words fits with children's need for active learning experiences that are concrete and accessible to various developmental levels.

"Through these cooperative experiences in reading, interpreting, and writing messages, children are developing beginning reading and writing abilities. They are also learning… about the usefulness of written communication and its contribution to the well-being of the community." (Gainsley & Lucier, 2001, p. 161).

crete anchor in real experiences); some children are able to anticipate "tomorrow." Young children can also best understand the pattern of their week as defined by "home days" and "school days." Individual pre-schoolers will exhibit various levels of understanding of even these simple time concepts and the words attached to them. Children learn time concepts most effectively if they consistently hear references to them in a meaningful context. So it's important to talk with them about what will happen today and tomorrow and to encourage them to recall recent events. Create a picture chart that shows home and school days and attach representations of upcoming events. You can refer to the chart when discussions of the future extend further than "tomorrow." Avoid quizzing children about the days of the week or the month. If adults say "What day is it?" or "What month is it?" children may fail at these closed-ended questions and become discouraged. Instead, simply state "Today is Monday" or "The month is May."

Departure Time (Pickup Time)

Preparing to leave the program at the end of a morning or afternoon session, or a full day, is the final transition of the day. Many factors affect the departure transition: what children are doing when it is time to go, how they are feeling (tired, hungry, confused), how many tasks need to be accomplished in preparation for leaving, and even the type of transportation that children will use to go home.

Departure-time guidelines

Here are some ideas for routines and procedures that will help you end the session on a positive note.

✔ *Warn children that pickup time is near.*

About 15 minutes before the session ends, give children a warning that it is almost time for them to be picked up. Or, if a goodbye gathering (see below) is a part of your program, let children know that this gathering is about to begin. You can use a large salt or sand timer to give children a clear visual reminder of how long they have before departure time begins.

✔ *If children are departing from inside, consider engaging in a regular large-group gathering at the end of the day.*

Use a variety of activities to hold children's interests. Activities may include informally talking about the day, singing a goodbye song together, playing an alliteration or rhyming game (similar to one used at arrival time) to say goodbye to each child, and/or reversing the attendance board process by taking photos off the board and placing them back in a storage container.

Salt timers are one way to give a clear visual signal that departure time is near.

✔ **If possible, plan to be outside just before departure, informing parents of procedures for children's safe departure.**

If an outdoor play time can be planned for the end of the day, departures go smoothly because children are already dressed, their belongings are gathered, and they can leave directly from the playground area. If departure is from an outdoor area, be sure that there is clear communication about the responsibility for the child passing to the parent, ensuring that the child is supervised through the departure process. Inform parents of your expectations about this *in writing*. For example, the policy may be that the parent is in charge of the child as soon as the parent has arrived on the playground and has greeted the child.

✔ **Record departures.**

If children are being picked up directly from the program (rather than taken by bus), devise a method for keeping track of who has left. This might be done by having the parent fill out a sign-out sheet posted by the door or gate, or sign out in person with one of the adults (if the group is outside).

✔ **Supervise bus pickups.**

If children are leaving by bus, be sure to provide adequate adult supervision as children move to the bus. Buses can initially be scary for small children. Adults need to be available to reassure children about what is happening. Adults should also be prepared to make any waiting time go smoothly. Having a list of waiting time activities and songs posted in a convenient place can help avoid chaos if buses are unexpectedly late. (See Chapter 4 for suggestions, especially p. 78.) "The Wheels

Having outside time right before departures allows children to finish up their activities as family members chat with teachers.

on the Bus" is an example of a fun song that would certainly be suited for this type of wait!

✔ *Educate parents about departure-time difficulties.*

Adults arriving to pick up children are often in a hurry. Consequently, they sometimes expect their children to instantly stop their activities and be ready to leave. Many children do greet their parents enthusiastically and are immediately ready to go. However, children can be glad to see a parent *and* still not want to leave, at least not right away. If adults demand immediate compliance, the situation can easily escalate into an emotional and time-consuming incident.

If a child is not ready to leave immediately, encourage parents to take these steps: if the child is still deeply involved in an activity, acknowledge the child's feelings about having to leave, describe the problem, give a time warning, and ask the child to help figure out a way (not when) to leave. If the child does not offer any suggestions, describe the choices for the child. You can educate parents about these strategies in a conversation, parent meeting, or handout (see the appendix for a reproducible handout). Be sure parents understand that the child cannot go back into the classroom and re-engage in activities, which would prolong the departure.

Another problem that sometimes arises at departure times is illustrated by the story of Suzanna, above. Many children do not leave with the same

Instead of ignoring children's feelings of confusion at departure times and demanding obedience...

...parents can take a few minutes to notice what their child is doing, share in his or her enthusiasm about the day's activities, and then problem-solve together.

"I know it's hard to go when you're having fun on the treehouse. Can you think of a fun way to come down the stairs?"

person each day; this can be confusing and upsetting for children. In such situations parents and teachers need to work together to find an individual solution for the child.

In Suzanna's case, the note with the symbol gave her something important: control of the information. By sharing the car pool driver's identity in a way that was appropriate for Suzanna's stage of "reading" and giving her control by placing the information in her lunchbox, the adults informed and reassured Suzanna in a way that met her need for concrete information at a predictable time.

Classroom-to-Classroom Transitions

Many programs have multiple classrooms for different age groups. In these programs children may begin in a classroom for toddlers and eventually join a classroom for three- and/or four-year-olds. While these may appear to be easy transitions since children remain in the same program and building, such moves involve major changes for children, who must adjust to new teachers or caregivers, new playmates, and a new room arrangement. Classroom adults therefore need to fully prepare children for the move, easing them in stages into the new classroom. A helpful approach for caregivers is to plan as if they were preparing the child to move to a new "home," taking into consideration all the things usually done when a family moves and keeping in mind, too, that this move includes a change in "family members"! Following are some ideas and strategies that will help children to get to know their new classroom:

Guidelines for room changes

✔ *Inform parents about the move.*

Prepare the parents for the transition as you prepare the child. Give them a handout about the new classroom, describing any differences in the daily routine of the classroom and any policy or other differences from the previous room. Let them know how the transition will take place. Introduce adults to the new classroom prior to the child's moving.

✔ *While you are preparing the family for the move, begin to prepare the child.*

Explain to the child that he or she will be moving on to a new classroom since he or she is getting older (or other reasons). Let the child know that you will be visiting the new classroom together, and do this on the same day that you tell him or her about the upcoming change. Making this visit right away gives the child concrete information that will help him or her understand more clearly what will happen. Make the first visit very brief, with family or a trusted caregiver staying with the child.

✔ *Arrange for the child to make a series of visits to the new classroom, going at different times in the daily routine over a period of about two weeks.*

If the child is able to stay independently, without the trusted caregiver, keep the stay brief (30–45 minutes). Be sure to include a mealtime in the sequence of visits if the child will be staying for meals. Discuss these visits with the child, naming and fully accepting any feelings of worry or resistance. Listening attentively to any concerns will assist the child's adjustment.

✔ *Make sure the child is introduced to other children in the new room.*

These introductions may take place at a large-group time, but they are even more important as the child encounters individual children during play. Adults should be sure to say children's names often, both the new child's and those of the other children.

✔ *As the time of the final move approaches, prepare the child's "space" in the new classroom.*

On visits to the classroom, adults can show the child a cubby with his or her symbol and name, the table where he or she will sit for small-group times, and possibly, a labeled cot.

✔ *After the child has made five or six visits during different parts of the day, arrange for a half-day visit to the classroom.*

This sets the stage for the final move. Ideally, the child will tell the adults he or she is ready to become a member of the new classroom. If the child does not choose the time for the final move, help him or her anticipate what day it will happen by using a visual reminder, such as a special picture on the calendar or a set of two or three small balloons that can be popped (one for each day, with the last one popped on the day of the move).

When adults provide both emotional support and concrete experiences to prepare children as they move to new classrooms, the distress that can result from changes that are unexpected or too rapid can be avoided. While it may seem time-consuming or complicated to provide such support, it helps the child maintain emotional balance and trust in the caregivers in the program. It can be much more difficult and time-consuming to re-establish such trust once it is lost. Careful attention to these classroom-to-classroom transitions can sustain the emotional well-being of the transitioning child as well as maintain the emotional stability of the classroom community the child is joining.

Moving on to Kindergarten (or Other Programs)

Guidelines for preparing children for kindergarten

Making the transition from prekindergarten to kindergarten, or from one child care setting to another, can be a very exciting *and* frightening experience for young children. Children often have been with an early childhood caregiver for as long as two or three years, sometimes starting in infancy. Consequently, these transitions require careful planning and preparation so children have the support they need to separate from their trusted caregivers and adjust to a whole new program.

✔ *Prepare children for the new program in several steps.*

The first step is to let children know that a change is coming and describe how that change will take place. Next, have children participate in activities that will help them get to know the new physical space they will be moving to as well as the adults in the new setting. These steps involve planning ahead *before* you inform children of the upcoming change so that you and the parents are ready to answer the questions that children may ask. Although you will need to plan carefully to devise prekindergarten activities and strategies, the most important aspect of planning is to prepare yourself and parents for the varied emotional reactions that children will have to the news of the change. Though there will be logistical details to communicate to children, the critical message to convey is that you will be there to support them every step of the way.

After many preparations, both at home and at preschool, this child is ready to step on the kindergarten bus. Successful early transitions build strength and confidence for all those yet to come.

✔ *Be prepared at all times to accept, acknowledge, and show understanding of children's feelings of uncertainty and worry.*

Children are very much in need of support, flexibility, and understanding as they adjust to the move to kindergarten or another program. The strategies for acknowledging children's feelings at departure times are also useful when children express strong feelings about the upcoming move to kindergarten (see pp. 16–17). You can educate parents about ways they can support children who are leaving for kindergarten by using the parent handout given in the appendix. See the sidebar on p. 34 for a list of children's books about this transition.

Activities and strategies for the kindergarten transition

Following are some ideas for supporting children both logistically and emotionally at this critical time. Most of these ideas apply to all program transitions, but some apply specifically to children leaving for kindergarten.

Advance information. Inform children one or two months before the transition begins so that they have time to explore the idea and ask questions about what will happen. A simple chart or "calendar" with pictures or symbols to show the number of days remaining can be helpful. This can be as simple as a paper chain made of 30 links with one removed each school day.

Program visit. Plan an outing to the new classroom. This may be arranged by the child's teachers or parents, or it may be a standard part of the local kindergarten's orientation plans. Many schools set up one or two visiting days for preschoolers.

It is best for children's first visit to the setting to take place when there are not a lot of other children in the space. Otherwise, the new children may be overwhelmed and distracted and they may not observe the new space as fully as they need to. On these visits, it is also important for children to meet the adults who will be their teachers. Consider taking photos on this visit and making them into a book that can be looked at and discussed frequently.

Kindergarten books. In the weeks leading up to the kindergarten transition, give children "kindergarten books" (notebooks or pads) to do "kindergarten work." Suggest simple things to do in the books that are suitable to their developmental levels, for example, encouraging them to write or draw in their own ways. This will give children a sense that they can manage the new tasks that are ahead of them; be sure the suggested tasks are easy.

Kindergarten area. Provide a "kindergarten space," where children can engage in playful "school" activities, for example, practicing letters and numbers, writing a letter or drawing a picture for their kindergarten teacher, "reading" to each other, and/or pretending about kindergarten. Such a space will give children the chance to explore through play some of their thoughts, feelings, and questions about kindergarten.

Goodbye card. Make a "goodbye card" during the final weeks before departure. This might include a group photo, a photo of the child doing a favorite activity in the classroom, and the child's dictation about what they liked about being in the preschool program. Adults can display these cards and hand them to children on their final day of school as a clear sign that the transition to the new setting is beginning.

A wall display says goodbye to preschoolers who are moving on.

Books to Support Children in Making Transitions to a New Program

Starting School by Janet Ahlberg.

This book includes humorous descriptions of the first day at school, then the first week, continuing up to Christmas.

The School by John Burningham.

Ilustrations and just a few words show what a child can expect at school.

Look Out Kindergarten, Here I Come by Nancy Carlson.

Enthusiastic Henry can hardly wait to start kindergarten. But will he still feel that way when he gets there?

Born in the Gravy by Denys Caznet.

Margarita, a Mexican-American girl, tells her father all about her first day of kindergarten.

Bill and Pete by Tomie DePaola.

William Everett Crocodile learns to write his name with the help of Pete, his toothbrush.

I Don't Want To! by Sally Grindley.

Jim mightily resists going to school, but by the end of the first day, he doesn't want to leave.

Spot Goes to School (Spot Va a La Escuala) by Eric Hill.

Spot, the pup, has fun at school with his friends.

When You Go to Kindergarten by James Howe.

This photo essay shows what a kindergarten class is like.

Alice Ann Gets Ready for School by Cynthia Jabar.

Alice Ann is so excited about her first day of school that she's the first one up and ready to go.

Froggy Goes To School by Jonathan London.

Froggy's nightmare about school does not come true, and he ends up having a good first day.

School by Emily McCully.

In a wordless story, a curious young mouse left at home sneaks off to see her older sibling's school.

The Kissing Hand by Audrey Penn.

A popular story suggests a way to deal with the separations of going to school.

Oliver Pig at School by Jean Van Leeuwen.

During Oliver Pig's first day at school, he builds with blocks, plays, and makes a friend.

The Night Before Kindergarten by Natasha Wing.

Verses in the manner of "The Night Before Christmas" encourage the reader who may be anxious about kindergarten.

Group photo. Take a group photo of the child's class with the teachers. This does not need to be professionally done — a snapshot is fine. Give copies to all the children. Post a copy in the classroom to stimulate discussions about the transition.

Goodbye celebration. Plan an ending occasion that includes parents and children. A adult-style "graduation" ceremony for children going on to kindergarten is *not* recommended; usually these are designed to please parents and are not developmentally appropriate (too much sitting and waiting, too abstract for young children). When adults plan "graduations" based on the rituals used with older children and young adults, children can spend the last weeks of the program in teacher-directed rehearsals that do not meet young children's emotional or developmental needs. Instead, plan a child-oriented event that is playful and fun — a celebration of the transition. This might be a family picnic or an open house in which families can come to see children's work (the "goodbye cards" may be displayed) and enjoy refreshments and a fun activity, one that does not require rehearsals and performances. For example, families could work on an art project together, such as making a special "kindergarten" hat or other project; watch a puppet show about going to a new school; or view a slide show set to music of all the children at play during the past year.

Return visits. Inform parents that you are open to return visits from children after they have adjusted to their new programs. When children have attended a preschool program for some time, their caregivers are often like a second family. Sometimes parents are afraid that return visits will result in children wanting to go back to their preschool. In reality, this is highly unlikely. Usually, children are reassured by the contact with previous caregivers, who have otherwise "disappeared," possibly creating concern. On such visits, they may also see that many of their old friends are no longer there — most will have moved onto kindergarten as well. Having access to trusted caregivers reaffirms that they are on solid ground as they reach out to new people.

●◞

The daily transitions to and from home and school and the transitions to kindergarten and other new programs are particularly challenging because young children are oriented to the here and now, which is tangible, rather than the future, which they can't see or touch. Teachers, caregivers, and parents have to work hard to help children grasp the meaning of "five minutes," "later today," "tomorrow," "next week," or "next month," finding concrete ways to communicate timing and the sequence of events. This will reassure children in transition, helping them to develop a solid base of independent skills and relationships as they encounter new experiences. They will encounter frequent transitions as they grow up; this early practice will prepare them for the inevitable changes that will occur throughout their lives.

Top Tips: Orientation, Arrivals and Departures, Room-to-Room and Kindergarten Transitions

- **Create an orientation period** for easing children into the program and daily routine. This might include a home visit, an open house, and short first days.

- **Establish routines for daily arrivals and departures, both for the group as a whole and individual children.** Support children by helping them predict, in a simple but specific way, what will happen at these times.

- **Make plans for drop-off and pickup times with parents.** Inform them of strategies for supporting their child during these times; help them understand the child's perspective. Involve them in developing individual routines for their child.

- **Be prepared to acknowledge children's feelings** if they have difficulty as they separate from parents or family members.

- **Have adequate staff available** at the beginning of the school year, so that each child can be greeted sensitively as he or she arrives and extra support can be provided to individual children who are upset.

- **Prepare individual spaces for children to store their belongings.** Label these spaces with the child's letter link or personal symbol and a family photo.

- **Plan for activities that will routinely begin and end the day.** These may include using an attendance chart, reading the message board, breakfast routines, singing special greeting and goodbye songs, departure activities, sign-out procedures, and so forth.

- **Plan a transition period as children prepare to leave the program for kindergarten or another classroom.** This might include a visit to the new program or other special activities.

- **Take a problem-solving approach** to daily arrivals and departures, and transitions to and from the program. There are many ways to support children and their parents if adults problem-solve together with them, looking for solutions to transition challenges.

3

Moving Through the Daily Routine: "Between Times" Can Be Learning Times

This chapter discusses the "between times" in the daily routine when children go to and from small- and large-group times, outside times, and rest times. These times are opportunities both to encourage learning and to ease the stress of shifting from one type of activity to another.

Each "between time" has its own unique set of circumstances; the transitions to and from small- and large-group times can be facilitated with simple movement activities, in contrast to the multiple tasks necessary at the beginnings of outside time or rest time. When thoughtfully planned, all these transitions can be occasions for learning in specific content areas; for example, children can step slowly to slow music while going to the planning table (movement and time concepts), repeat a favorite nursery rhyme while moving to the large-group meeting place (language and literacy, movement concepts), or count their classmates as they arrive at small-group time (math concepts). By including such activities, adults can encourage new ways of thinking and new skills.

One of the most important benefits of planning transitions carefully, in addition to the increase in learning time, is that the emotional tone of the day becomes positive and balanced. Children are very susceptible to the upsets of others; even when they are not directly involved, they readily absorb anxiety or frustration from their peers. Reducing transition difficulties for two or three children results in more relaxing time for everyone. A program that flows easily from one activity period to another is a joy both for caregivers and children. When children are happy and having fun, they learn more effectively and maintain a higher level of motivation throughout the day.

Guidelines for "Between-Times" Transitions

✔ Plan and maintain a consistent daily routine.

Smooth transitions depend on children's familiarity with the daily routine, so it is essential to plan a predictable routine that becomes the foundation for children as they move through the day. Since children understand time through obvious physical clues, such as seeing teachers setting up for breakfast or hearing a familiar song, the daily routine becomes the child's "clock." Each component is part of a pattern that helps children predict what will happen next. Adults can support this by keeping the daily routine as consistent as possible and supporting awareness of the different parts of the daily routine.

✔ Post a daily routine chart.

One tool that helps children learn the routine and stay "on track" as activities change is a daily routine chart, which provides a concrete visual representation of the routine for children. The components of a daily routine can be depicted in a variety of ways. Each segment can be represented by a photograph or symbol; these are then placed in order to show the sequence of the day. This set of pictures or symbols can be placed in a book and/or made into a wall display posted at children's eye level. If there is room on a wall or the back of a storage unit, it can be particularly helpful to display the routine horizontally so it can be "read" from left to right. Some programs display their daily routine components like train cars, making the length of each "car" proportional to the length of that component, for example, a short car for a 10-minute planning time and a long car for a 60-minute choice time. Daily routine displays or books should be available at all times so that children may refer to them throughout the day.

✔ Give warning signals as needed.

Another way to reinforce children's awareness of the parts of the routine is to give a warning signal five or ten minutes before the next activity starts and then to signal again at the start of the activity. Teachers or children can give verbal warnings to individuals and small groups. When the warning period is over, the beginning of a transition might be signaled by

Daily routine charts use words and pictures, drawings, or photos to let children know the sequence of the day's events. A clothespin (right) can be moved down the chart to indicate what part of the routine is happening.

playing a musical instrument, starting a special song, or distributing materials to be used during the transition activity. Such warnings are common at the end of work time; they may also be used near the end of small-group time or outside time — any time children are absorbed in their activities. Knowing what to expect can make it easier for children to make the transition to the next activity. (See the discussion of cleanup time, p. 89, for more on warning signals.)

Children or adults can warn others of upcoming changes in the routine by ringing a bell, flipping a light switch, or using other sensory cues.

✔ ***Understand and plan for various kinds of transitions.***

Each transition time has unique characteristics and requirements. Some transitions require only a simple activity that acts as a bridge, such as having children move like a favorite animal as they go from a large-group activity to their usual small-group-time meeting place. Other transitions, such as the preparations for lunch or outside time, involve a bit more planning, perhaps requiring the teacher to prepare such visual props as a "helper chart," a picture sequence for putting on winter clothing, or a "Simon Says" puppet ("Simon says, 'Put on your snowpants'").

Activity Ideas and Support Strategies for Particular Transitions

In addition to the general daily routine strategies just discussed, there are many specific ideas and strategies you can use to help children move to and from particular parts of the daily routine. These ideas are given in the sections that follow. Many of these ideas can also be used during other parts of the day, with minor adjustments or changes. Include children in making these adjustments,

One aspect of planning for transitions is to prepare visual props that aid children's independence, such as the helper chart directly above and the pocket chart at left. The pocket chart is used by children as they leave their planning table to start their work-time activity. Children put a nametag in a pocket labeled with the name and symbol of the area they have decided to play in.

since they usually enjoy choosing transition activities once they have become familiar with the sequence of the day. Often they will think of creative variations on the adult's strategy, re-energizing the group and extending the strategy to everyone's delight.

Moving to the message board or helper chart

Some programs begin the day with a large-group meeting, moving perhaps from breakfast or a post-arrival free play period to the formal beginning of the day. Activities such as "reading" message boards (see Chapter 2, p. 24) and choosing the day's "helpers" are often included in this meeting. Following are some ideas for the transitions to these opening activities.

Helper chart transition song. The "A Helper I Will Be" song can be used to cue children to gather around the helper chart. The adult begins the song and children join in:

> (To the tune of "The Farmer in the Dell")
>
> A helper I will be,
>
> A helper I will be,
>
> Hi-ho the derry-o,
>
> A helper I will be.

Repeat until all the children have come to sit in front of the helper chart.

Message board transition song. This variation on the previous strategy can be used to signal that it is time to read the message board together:

> (To the tune of "If You're Happy and You Know It")
>
> Put your bottom on the floor, on the floor,
>
> Put your bottom on the floor, on the floor,
>
> Put your bottom on the floor and read the message board,
>
> Put your bottom on the floor, on the floor.

Arriving at large-group time

Often adults tell children that it is time for a large-group activity, then wait for everyone to "look ready" or "sit still" before starting the first song or game. Being still is developmentally very difficult for young children, and insisting on it often makes the problem worse. Avoiding this waiting period and getting started right away with an interesting activity (preferably one that includes choices of new words or actions) can be much more effective — children will want to join the fun. (See illustrations on pp. 42–43.) The following songs are effective examples; they include lively music as well as choices. These ideas are provided as quick starters for large groups; they are short, easy-to-join action songs and chants that will attract children to the gathering and engage them right away. As you plan for this first activity, decide if you need a long or a short activity. For example, as you wait for children who need extra time to clean up after a small group, longer activities or songs, such as "Heart to Heart" ("Corazón a Corazón"), may be suitable. Choose songs and movements children already know and enjoy.

"Mi Cuerpo Hace Musica" ("I Have Music Inside Me"). This is an action song about various parts of the body and what they do, as in this verse:

> My mouth says la, la, la.
> My hands say (clap, clap, clap)
> My feet say, ta, ta, ta. (tap feet)
> My waist and hips say...
> (Spoken: Are you ready?)
> Cha, cha, cha. Cha, cha, cha.
> My waist and hips say cha, cha, cha.
> Cha, cha, cha.
> My waist and hips say cha, cha, cha.*

Begin the song in Spanish as children are arriving, then sing it in English. Then repeat the Spanish and English versions, asking the children for other movements for the hands, feet, or other parts of the body, such as shoulders or toes.

Nursery rhymes. Using a "spider pat," tap your legs slowly and silently for a minute or so, setting up a steady beat. Then chant to the beat (italic idicates accented syllables):

> *Lit*tle Miss *Muf*fet sat on a tuffet,
> *Eat*ing an *ice* cream *cone* __,
> *A*long came a *spi*der and *dangled* be*side* her,
> She *told* him to *go* get his *own*
>   __.
> (from *The New Adventures of Mother Goose: Gentle Rhymes for Happy Times,* Bruce Lansky, 1999, p. 8)

"Sitting in the Soup." This song about the lively ingredients in a pot of soup will bring children running to your large group

Visual Props Provide Reassurance

Kaylani begins to cry as children sit down for afternoon snack. "I want my Mommy," she whispers between sobs. Her teacher kneels by her, gently stroking her back, "You're feeling really sad, Kaylani. You're missing your mom." Kaylani nods and begins to calm. Her teacher then suggests that they go look at the daily routine chart to see when her mother will be coming. Together they find the photo of afternoon snack time and notice that it is followed by small-group time, outside time, and pickup time. Kaylani smiles as she looks at the photos, realizing she is now more able to predict when she will see her mom. Seeing pictures of the sequence of events leading to her mother's return is much more reassuring then simply being told about it, because it fits her developmental need to understand the day in a concrete way.

*From Linking Up [book and CD] (p. 242), by Sarah Pirtle, 1998, Cambridge, MA: Educators for Social Responsibility. ©1998 Educators for Social Responsibility and Sara Pirtle. Reprinted with permission.

Insisting that children "look ready" and "sit still" at the beginning of large-group time can create more disruption than readiness. So instead of saying "I'm waiting until you are ready"...

...consider beginning with an easy-to-join activity or song that will immediately attract and engage children as they arrive at the large-group space. Let children join in at their own pace.

to shake like salt, twist like peppers, and jump like beans! As children come to the large-group area, sing the first phrase of the song slowly to build suspense for the actions that will come next: "Here we are sitting in the soup, sitting in the soup on Sunday." (You can change Sunday to the actual day of the week.) Then sing enthusiastically, as children stand to move, "Nowww! Shake yourself like salt..." Sing the bridge (which gives time for movement and then helps settle children to sitting again): "The beans are jumping in the pot...," slowing down as you get to "Come back a-giggle on home," to encourage children to sit down. Repeat "Come back a-giggle on home" until everyone is sitting. (For the complete song, see Pirtle, 1998, p. 73.)

"Sitting in the Soup" variation. Instead of "Now! Shake yourself like salt," ask children what foods (or other things) they like a lot. Then sing this phrase to the music of "Now! Shake..." using these words instead:

> Ohh, I like **strawberries** (peaches/my dog/dancing, etc.)
> a lot.
>
> I like **strawberries** a lot.
>
> You ask me what I like a lot?
>
> Oh, I like **strawberries** a lot.

"The Colors of Earth." This song encourages children to notice the range of colors in nature and to connect this with the diversity of human beings (see lyrics below). Sing this song as children are arriving at large group. Stop at the end, and ask the children to wave to or shake hands with someone next to them and look into the person's eyes and say what they see. They may say the name of a color or they may say something more symbolic like "the sky" or "the ocean." Accept whatever ideas they contribute; in time they may associate colors with other things as the song inspires them to do.

> **Chorus**
> We are made of the colors of earth.
> Each color is different.
> Each color is true.
> We are made of the colors of earth.
> I love the colors that made you.

> **Verse 1**
> When I look in the eyes of my friends,
> I can see topaz, I can see sky.
> The green and the gray of the sea
> Rolling by and the dazzling
> brown river in the morning.

Verse 2

When I look at the hands of my friends,

I can see chestnut, I can see corn.

The color of wheat fields and a dappled brown fawn,

And the rain-kissed black trees in the morning.*

"Heart to Heart"/"Corazón a Corazón." This is a song about how feelings affect us, for example, "Sometimes I feel angry, I don't want to hit or shout," or "Sometimes I feel scared, I don't want to hide away." As children are arriving, begin this song with the variation "Sometimes I feel happy, I want to smile and laugh," then follow this with the "real" words "Sometimes I feel scared, I don't want to hide away." Once children have the idea, ask them to sing the song by naming feelings and saying what they want to do when they feel that way. (See Pirtle, 1998, p. 184.)

"Where Is Thumbkin?" This is a popular preschool song, sung to the tune of "Frère Jacques/Are You Sleeping." For this version silently hold your thumbs up, then put them behind your back and begin to sing, "Where is Thumbkin?" After singing one time through, add in the name of a child you are waiting for: "Where is Ella?" Hopefully she'll arrive saying, "Here I am!" Encourage the group to sing happily in response, "Here she is!"

"We Are Waiting." Here's a similar idea that doesn't use the thumbs:

(To the tune of "Frère Jacques"/"Are You Sleeping")

We are waiting, we are waiting,

For our friends, for our friends,

To come to our circle, to come to our circle,

Here comes (child's name), here comes (child's name).

"We Are Waiting" variation" (for attendance).

Who is missing, who is missing,

Can you guess, can you guess?

I'm not going to tell you, I'm not going to tell you,

Look around, look around.

"Clap Your Hands."

(To the tune of "Row, Row, Row Your Boat")

Clap, clap, clap your hands,

Clap your hands for (child's name).

Here he comes to join us,

Clap your hands for (child's name).

Wiggle, wiggle, wiggle your toes,

Wiggle your toes for (child's name).

Here she comes to join us,

Wiggle your toes for (child's name).

*From *Linking Up* [book and CD] (p. 46), by Sarah Pirtle, 1998, Cambridge, MA: Educators for Social Responsibility.
©1998 Educators for Social Responsibility and Sara Pirtle. Reprinted with permission.

Ask children for other ideas about what to move as each new child approaches.

"Fandagumbo" or "Pizza." Begin singing one of these songs (both are on the CD *Fandagumbo,* Julie Austin, 1999) and move to the song. Ask the children to make up movements. Repeat the song until everyone has arrived.

Surprise bag. Bring to the large-group space a "circle-time bag" that contains objects you will use during the large-group activity, such as a special puppet, song cards, or other interesting objects. Hold an object so it is partway out of the bag, and ask children to guess what it is. If the surprise object is a puppet, ask for and try out children's ideas for "waking up the puppet."

Story tin. Bring to the large-group space a special cookie tin with objects for a story you will make up together. As you wait for children to gather, ask them to guess what's in the tin.

Leaving large-group time

Departing from large-group activities smoothly, without a stampede, requires a simple activity or strategy. The following ideas are to facilitate those times that children need to move from large group to the coatroom, bathroom, or into smaller groups. Children respond enthusiastically to any activity that is playful and active, even if the enjoyment is watching the reaction of others to the activity. If slowing down the departure of children is important, such as for hand washing, choose an activity that allows you to adjust the timing of the departure, such as the first song below.

"Llego la Hora"/"Now's the Time." Sing this song about transitions through once, then change the repeating phrase to include a child's name and the activity he or she is going to, for example,

> Now's the time for *Roberto* to go,
>
> For Roberto to go, for Roberto to go.
>
> Now's the time for Roberto to go,
>
> Now is the time for hand washing.

(The song, by Roberto Diaz, is available in Pirtle, 1998, p. 103.)

Passing a beanbag and freezing on signal is a fun way to decide who's next to leave large group.

The adult joins in as children find creative ways to leave large-group time.

Depending on how much time is needed between children, sing the song again, with the first phrase, "Now the time for hand washing has come," perhaps adding a spider pat each time on a part of the body children have chosen.

"ABC Song." Sing "A-B-C-D-E-F. *F* is for ____? Yes, Frank and Fran. They can go get ready for lunch!" Start again: "A-B-C-D-E-F-G. *G* is for ____? Yes, George and Galen can get ready for lunch," and so on.

"Fee, fie, fo" name game. "Fee, fie, fo, /f/ ____? Yes, **F**rank can go to wash his hands. Bee, bi, bo, /b/ ____? Yes, **B**etseida and **B**ob can go wash their hands," and so on.

Pass the ball. Begin to pass a ball or a beanbag, counting aloud with each pass until the leader (an adult or child) says "Freeze." Whoever has the ball then passes the ball on and leaves for the next activity. The game continues. The leader is the last person and puts the ball away.

"Pass the ball" variations. Instead of counting, sing a favorite song or say the alphabet, one letter for each pass, and pass the ball until the leader says "Freeze."

Stepping stones. Prepare seven or eight cardboard "stones" and ask children to color them. Laminate them if possible. Arrange a path of stones from the space where you are to the area you are going to next (sink, bathroom, and so forth).

Duck, duck, goose. Choose a child leader, and pass a beanbag, a stuffed animal, or a yarn ball; ask everyone to say "Duck, duck, duck, duck" with the child leader, until the leader says "Goose!" The leader then leaves the group (instead of chasing the "goose"), the "goose" becomes the new leader, and so on.

Speckled frog. Set up five chairs on the edge of the large-group-time rug, and select some of the children to sit in them. Sing "Speckled Frog." After each child "jumps" into the "pool," he or she hops to the next

A combination of words and pictures support children as they sing this familiar song.

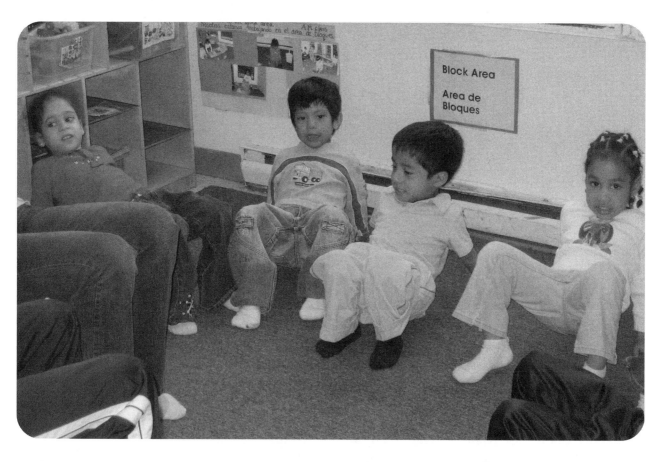

After singing a favorite song, children begin a series of yoga poses to transition from large-group time to going out-doors. During the stretching poses they stand up and leave one by one to get their coats.

activity. As chairs empty, they are refilled by more children until everyone has played the game and left the large-group area.

Transition using an idea from large group. Use a character, action, or words from one of the large-group activities to support children in moving to the next activity. For example, after moving to the "Popcorn" song (see the CD *Rhythmically Moving 7*, 2003), ask two or three children at a time to "pop hop" to the next activity while everyone else pops in place. Or ask children to move to the next activity like their favorite animal from a story you have been reading with the group.

Having each child get out his or her own set of materials eases the transition to small-group time.

Leaving small-group time

Once adults have begun to use transition strategies regularly to support children who are changing activities, coming up with ideas can be a spontaneous response related to what children have just been doing. These are often the most effective strategies for motivating interest in the transition. The following ideas all use information from play that has just occurred to create a bridge from the current activity to the next. All are appropriate to use after the five-minute warning has been given for the end of the activity.

Animated materials. Have one of the toy animals or people from the small-group time "talk" to the children, telling them what will happen next. If children have been working with small plastic bears and play dough, a bear might say, "I had a good time with the play dough today. Now it's time to go outside. Anyone who has blue bears like me can put their bears away and go to get their coat." Then pick up a yellow bear and say, "Now anyone who has two yellow bears like me can go put on their coat," and so on.

A Smooth Transition

After giving the warning that it is almost time to end a small-group time in which children have been counting as they add Velcro-backed dots to stuffed ladybugs, Debbie, the adult, asks the children to place dots on their ladybug while she closes her eyes. The children all begin to count and add dots to their ladybugs. After a couple of minutes, she opens her eyes and speaks with individual children: "Rosalyn, I see your ladybug has six dots. One, two, three, four, five, six. Where do you plan to play today?" Rosalyn puts the bugs and dots back in the bag and tells Debbie, "I'm going to make a dinosaur house for T-Rex. It's going to be big!" Debbie responds, "I'd like to see that when you're finished." Rosalyn heads off to the block area.

Recall. Each child shows and talks about what he or she made at small-group time and then goes to the next activity. (Note that all High/Scope programs have a recall time every day after work time. This recall after a group activity happens only occasionally and may not involve recalling by each child.)

Guess how many. Ask children to take turns guessing how many of the small-group materials are hiding in your hand. Each child guesses; counts what's there; and then goes to get ready for outside time, nap, or other activity.

Anyone who has ___? Play an attribute guessing game with the materials children have in front of them. For example, "Anyone who has something that is round (or red, bumpy, etc.) can put their materials away and go to the lunch table," or "Anyone who has curly hair (or blue eyes, red letters on their tee shirt, etc.)...."

"Anyone who has" variations. Use numbers or letters for guessing, for example, "Anyone who has something that starts with *B*" or "Anyone who has a stripe pattern (or three buttons, two sleeves, etc.) on their clothes...."

Recall gatekeeper. As children get up to leave, act out the role of gatekeeper, using your arm as the gate. Children arrive at the "gate" and the "gatekeeper" chants,

> Fee, fie, fo, fum,
>
> Small-group time is nearly done,
>
> Fee, fie, fo, fum,
>
> At small-group time, what did you do?

(The child describes something he or she did and the gate lifts.)

Guidelines for moving to outside time

This transition, which usually involves both toileting and dressing to go outside, can present many challenges as children try to accomplish all the self-care tasks involved and stay focused on what will happen next.

✔ *To set the stage for a smooth transition to the outdoor play area, prepare the coatroom or dressing area beforehand.*

Review the organization of open space and your storage places. Is there a space near the coats with enough room for children as a group to get dressed comfortably? Is it clear where each child's belongings are placed? Use children's letter links (name and letter-linked picture) or picture symbols on coat pegs and cubbies, and suggest to parents that these go on such items within the cubbies as lunchboxes, sunscreen, and boots.

✔ *Encourage toileting during the half hour previous to outside time.*

This will prevent a "pile-up" of children waiting by the bathroom door. Often children are very excited about going outside and do not choose to use the toilet. To engage these children, try "circling up" and starting an activity or song with those children who are waiting to use the toilet (for more on circling up, see Chapter 4). Children will be more likely to join in if waiting to use the toilet looks like good fun.

✔ *Plan what children will do as they wait for others to get on their outside clothes.*

For example, ask children to wait in an area where they can do puzzles, or sing a song with the group that is ready. Encourage children who are dressed to help other children with their clothing. If the location of your playground permits, avoid such waits altogether by stationing one adult outside and letting each child go out as soon as he or she is ready.

Activities and strategies for moving to outside time

Dressing charts. For dressing in seasonal clothing, make a dressing chart that shows the sequence for putting on clothing, for example, for outdoor winter activities, snowpants first, then boots, then a jacket, hat, and finally mittens; for summer water activities, a bathing suit, canvas or plastic shoes, sunscreen, and possibly a hat.

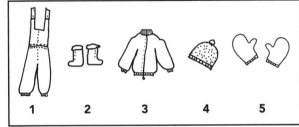

Dressing partners. Keep cards with children's names accompanied by their letter links or symbols in a box or envelope. Have children randomly pick out a name; this is their "dressing partner." Partners help each other get dressed.

Dressing places/blast-off pads. If children have not been successful at independently gathering their things from a coatroom and moving them to an area large enough for dressing, consider laying out children's clothing (perhaps in the area where their rest mats usually go), creating personal "blast-off pads." If they can carry all their things, ask them to take clothing to their "blast-off pads." Then the adult sings "We're Going Outside," starting with this verse:

> (To the tune of "Home on the Range")
> We're going outside!
> We're dressing in *coats and hats* (or
> > snowsuits and hats) too.
> When dressing is done, we'll blast off for
> > fun.
> We'll run all about, me and you.

Some children will join in with the song as they dress. As they finish dressing, they chant, "One, two, three, blast off!" and go to the door (emphasize the counting and engine noises of "blasting off").

Dressing song verse two. As children are dressing, you can help keep them interested in what will happen next by singing this second verse to "We're Going Outside":

> We're going outside!
> Where there are swings and bicycles, too.

Even if the dressing area is cramped, adults can support a smooth transition to the outdoors. This group plays a game while children dress by their cubbies, so children do not become bored as they wait to go. Adults participate at the children's level.

This dressing area is well organized with personal cubbies for children's belongings and coat hooks labeled with children's names and letter links.

We'll play in the sand, and we'll go hand in hand,
We'll run all about, me and you.

(You can change the words "swings and bicycles" to other current favorite outside activities.)

Waiting circles. If some pairs are all ready to go, have them wait by the door at the "waiting circle" (indicated by letters, symbols, or animals on the floor) and ask them to sing "We're Going Outside" or another song of their choice. Keep this waiting circle as short as possible.

Rest-time routines

Rest time presents extra challenges for children and adults because it is often a required part of the day's routine and it sometimes does not match the wants or needs of individual children. Some children are truly ready for a nap at this time and some are not. Adults need to make a plan for this time period that will support all children, not just the tired ones. If adults give choices as children transition from the busy stimulation of the day to the reduced activity and quiet of rest time, children are more likely to succeed in adjusting to expectations.

The investment of time you make in planning for and supporting the transition to rest or quiet activity can result in a true rest for everyone. The following ideas and strategies will help adults support the wide variety of children's needs that must be considered during rest time.

Guidelines for rest time

✔ *Set mats or cots out in consistent positions.*

This will help children to anticipate rest time and adjust to the habits of those around them. Occasionally the locations may need to be changed as children find certain locations too noisy (due to another child, a busy entrance, and so forth).

✔ *Make a "cot map" that shows the position of the individual cots or mats throughout the room.*

Post it near the rest area. The map can help staff maintain a consistent environment for children if there are substitutes or staff changes. On the map, include symbols children know (their letter links or personal symbols and the interest area symbols), and post the map at children's eye level so children can "read" it as well. Children like joining into the cot distribution process, either by being "cot helpers" for the adults or by taking their own cot to the place shown on the map. Using the cot map

With her cot located in the same place each day, this child feels secure as she drifts off to sleep.

will make rest time more predictable for children, helping them learn the location of their cot and contributing to their sense of control. (For more information on area symbols, see p. 95. For information on personal symbols or letter links, see p. 12.)

✔ *Help children predict what is expected by creating a rest-time routine and following it consistently.*

When this routine is repeated daily and the adults themselves remain quiet and calm, even active children can accept the restrictions of this part of the day, and perhaps even fall asleep.

A few minutes of warm support and attention from a familiar adult and the comfort of a special doll ease this child's transition to sleep.

At rest time, insisting that children do as they are told and fall asleep can make the problem worse and disrupt other children. Instead of ignoring children's difficulties...

...notice and describe the difficulties that you see. Take a problem-solving approach, trying to see the situation from the child's perspective, and find a way to help the child settle in.

✔ **Give a warning as the first step in your rest-time routine.**

For example, flash the lights and tell children: "Five [or ten] minutes until rest time!"

✔ **Once rest time begins, do not expect children to shift instantly from active to passive; plan a gradual slowdown.**

Before trying to complete other rest-time tasks such as cleaning or team planning, adults should be prepared to help children settle in for the first 20–30 minutes of rest time.

Your routine should consist of increasingly calmer "stages." Begin with a quiet activity. For example, have small baskets of toys or books available for children to take to their cots to play with. The next stage might be listening to a recorded story (on tape or CD) or to an adult reading a story without showing the pictures. Reading a "chapter book" like *Charlotte's Web* or *The Wonderful Wizard of Oz* can be very effective (as suggested by Benny in the story on p. 58). Use a calm and only slightly animated voice as you read. Be sure to let the children know that you will not be showing the pictures — you can compare the experience to listening to a story tape. The final stage might be playing quiet music. This can be a good time to expose children to diverse music that is calming and easy to listen to, such as soft guitar or flute music, lullabies, or quiet classical music.

✔ **Be clear and yet flexible about rest-time behavior.**

Remember that rest time is an adult-initiated required activity that is not needed by some children; this means that implementing it is the adult's problem, not the child's. Adults must respond, in whatever ways that are manageable for the group, to individual children's needs. For example, there may be differences in expectations from child to child. Demanding absolutely quiet behavior is not likely to result in a restful experience for you or the children. Some children may need to do quiet activities on their cot for the entire rest time.

✔ **Approach difficulties that arise with individual children by using problem-solving strategies.**

If problems persist over several rest times, speak to the child about the problem at some other time of the day. Ask the child to think of ideas that might help to make rest time easier. (See the story on p. 58 and the illustrations on pp. 54–55 for examples of rest-time problem solving.)

✔ **Give plenty of adult support for the first 15–20 minutes of rest time as the children settle in.**

If possible, ensure that each child has a few moments with an adult. Exchange a few quiet words, help the child become comfortable by offering a quick back rub, or just say a simple "good night." These small gestures can give the warm support a child needs to relax into rest or sleep. If any children become frustrated with the requirement to rest because they aren't able to sleep, be sure to acknowledge their feelings, "You're feeling frustrated (or mad) about having to rest. I know it seems long."

A Rest-Time Routine

1. Children enjoy a very active dance and then begin a "winding down" process.

2. Children play a "quieting" game, pretending to be cocoons.

3. The adult leads a game that plays on the letter sounds in children's names. As their sound comes up, the children leave the group one by one and go to set up their cot.

4. A teacher hands out bedding.

5. Children set up their special resting place.

6. Having gone through a routine they are comfortable with, children settle in happily.

Benny Solves an Adult Problem

It was near the beginning of the school year, and Benny had just turned five. It was rest time, but he had not needed a nap at home or at school since the previous spring. Because of state regulations, however, classroom adults had to require Benny to "rest" with the other children. During recent rest times, Benny had become more and more animated — flipping about on his mat, making squeaky noises, calling out to other children. It was Betsy's day to be with the children as they rested, and she was apprehensive. As children prepared their mats and picked out books, Benny alternately hopped about on one foot making funny noises and stretched out and rolled across the floor. He looked more like he was gearing up for a major athletic event than for a quiet rest. Sure enough, Betsy's apprehensions came true; rest time seemed interminably long as Benny noisily crawled up and down on his mat like a bed bug, making loud squeaks. Betsy's offers of back rubs and pleas for quiet only gave her brief respites of calm before the squeaking and wiggling began anew. In no time she was exhausted and frustrated.

Finally rest time ended, and children began to pack up their rest bags. Betsy went to where Benny was working on his bag and she offered to hold it open while he stuffed his mat into it. He handed her the bag and began to roll his mat. As Betsy pulled the bag open wide, she considered carefully how she would begin. Quietly Betsy told him, "Benny, I have a problem that I need to talk to you about." (It was, she realized, her problem. Benny was being asked to do something that was no longer developmentally appropriate for him; rest time did not meet his needs or wants in any way.)

"What problem?" he asked with sincere curiosity.

"I felt really frustrated during rest time today because noise and jumping around make it hard for the other children to rest." Benny had finished stuffing his bag. He pulled the cord tight and paused for a few seconds as he considered his answer.

"You know I shouldn't have to even do dumb rest 'cuz I'm five now."

"Ohhh…you think children who are five shouldn't have to rest. Boy, I wish I could change the rules about rest time, but the teachers don't get to make up all the rules that we have at school." (Betsy paused for a few seconds as she considered explaining to him about state licensing regulations, then quickly decided to keep it simple.) "You really don't like rest and I can't change the rules about rest. So what could we do to solve this? What could we do to make rest easier for you?"

Barely hesitating, Benny told her, "You could read chapter books. You know, like The Wizard of Oz, or those crow books."

"Oh yeah — we used to do that last year, didn't we? Sammy Jay [a chapter book about a bird's adventures Betsy sometimes read to preschoolers was one they had read]. So you think rest would be quieter if we read chapter books?"

"A lot!" Benny told Betsy emphatically.

"Wow — thanks for that idea, Benny! We'll try it tomorrow," she told him.

Benny took his bag to the rest mat cabinet and went off to play.

The next day Betsy sat amid the group of resting children; she told everyone that they would be reading a "chapter" book and that since they were resting their eyes, she would not be showing pictures. Betsy began:

"Sammy Jay…" The room grew still. A few pages into the book, Betsy glanced around as she read. The room was calm and quiet. Some children were dropping off to sleep, some were listening. Benny lay motionless on his mat, wide awake, with a look of complete absorption on his face. He had solved Betsy's problem and his own.

— From *You Can't Come to My Birthday Party! Conflict Resolution With Young Children* (pp. 216–218), by Betsy Evans, 2002, Ypsilanti, MI: High/Scope Press.

✔ *During rest time, be a model of calm and quiet for the children.*

If they are working or planning in another area of the room, adults should avoid using voices that can be heard across the room. If they are near the children, they should whisper to one another and to the children.

✔ *Make a simple representation of the rest-time routine.*

This is a portable chart that can be carried around the room and shared with children as they are settling in. The sequence of photos and/or drawings might include

- A photo of the time period just before rest time

- The five-minute warning, represented by the number 5

- Photos of mats or cots being set out and children taking books to their mats

- A photo of the tape or CD player symbolizing the beginning of a story or quiet music

- Last in the sequence, a photo of children resting quietly on their cots

✔ *If possible, provide a shortened rest time for children who need it.*

In some programs, if children have not fallen asleep after 45–60 minutes, they can put away their cots and select quiet activities in particular areas of the room until it is time for everyone to wake up. This is a more effective use of the children's learning time then leaving them fidgeting on their cots.

Preventing and Resolving Turn-Taking Issues

Turn-taking is a frequent form transitions take in the classroom, and yet it rarely receives special planning or attention. It can be very helpful if strategies for facilitating turn-taking can be considered in advance. This will prevent many conflicts over turns and help to resolve those that do occur.

Strategies and experiences for predictable turn-taking situations

When planning with classroom staff, think about situations that will require turns, such as choosing a song or book for large-group time, leading the group in circling up before moving to another space (see Chapter 4), or helping to set the table for lunch. These occasions happen frequently in classrooms and require special planning. Decide on what strategies and/or activities will be used to facilitate turns at these moments. The following are some ideas:

Clothespin list. Post a list of all the children's names and symbols on the wall, with a clothespin that moves down the list. This works well for predictable times when only one person can choose a song or a book.

Book of songs and fingerplays. Make a book of songs and fingerplays, with each on a page illustrated with a simple drawing and the

Symbols are moved across this turn-taking list to indicate whose turn it is.

It is this child's turn to pick a song from the class songbook. Children chant, "Zick-zack, what will she choose?" as they wait for her choice, then sing the song.

name of the song or activity. Putting the pages in plastic sheet covers ensures that the book will last all year. Two children can be asked to choose a song or fingerplay from the book while the others tap a steady beat and chant something simple, for example, "What will they choose, what will they choose, zicky-zack, zicky-zock, what will they choose." Repeat as needed.

Turn-taking cards. Make a box of cards with children's names and letter links or personal symbols that can be drawn from randomly (teachers set aside the names that have been picked until all names are drawn over the week). This works well for choices that come up spontaneously during large-group gatherings in which there may not be turns for everyone.

Sign-up list. Post a sign-up list for turns, using a dry-erase board with a marker or symbols and names in a basket that can be fastened to Velcro tabs to form a list of people waiting for a turn that shows the order of the turn. The name is erased or the name card removed when the turn is taken.

Helper chart. Create a "helper chart" for classroom tasks using a writing surface or pockets. To make choosing helpers easier, first make a list of "real" jobs (involving actual work that children can help with) such as setting the table, watering the plants, inspecting the room after cleanup, helping with problem solving, bringing in the milk cartons at snack time, feeding classroom pets, and so forth. Second, determine how the class will decide who will do these jobs. If possible, involve the children in your discussions about job names and the method of choosing helpers. Including them in these decisions will facilitate social problem-solving skills and heighten their level of co-operation with the plan.

Job charts may be created using Velcro tabs under the name of each job so that the child's name can be fastened under it. Fabric pockets may also be used; label each pocket with the job name and have name cards for the children that fit inside. (Each card should have a printed name

Cards labeled with children's names and letter links or symbols can be used as part of a turn-taking system and have many other uses as well.

plus the child's letter link or personal symbol.) The pocket-style job charts may take longer to make but will be more durable. You can put Velcro tabs on each pocket so the names of the jobs can change with the needs of the classroom.

Strategies for turn-taking conflicts

You will also need to have a consistent plan for how teachers and caregivers will respond when there is a conflict over turns with an object, a favorite space or activity, or other common classroom issues. It does not help children learn new skills if adults make judgments about who is "right" or "first" in turn-taking situations; this type of intervention only creates more dependence on adults to always solve problems. Also keep in mind that children are not being "bad" when they urgently want the first turn and are quite aggressive about trying to get it. While it is important to set limits on hurtful behaviors, it is also important to remember that young children are egocentric — at this developmental stage, it very hard for them to see the wants and needs of others. Adults can help them experience the rewards of turn-taking with others by facilitating a discussion of how this will happen, rather than forcing them to share. If sharing is not *chosen,* it is not truly sharing.

Using the problem-solving steps. After setting limits, facilitate problem solving by using the six High/Scope problem-solving steps listed in the sidebar. By using these steps you will not only help children find a solution to their immediate problem of how to share space or materials but also help them to build important social skills.

Avoiding number limits in play areas. Strategies are not included here for using turn-taking to limit the number of children using a given area of the classroom. Rules like "Only six people allowed at the block area" or "Only one child per computer" are not recommended in the

A helper chart with jobs that have real importance for the classroom is one way to make sure all children have a turn at the jobs they like.

Problem-Solving Steps

1. Approach calmly.
2. Acknowledge children's feelings.
3. Gather information.
4. Restate the problem.
5. Ask children for solutions.
6. Give follow-up support.

For more information on how to carry out these steps, see *You Can't Come to My Birthday Party! Conflict Resolution With Young Children* (Evans, 2002).

Rather than force children to share, adults can facilitate a problem-solving discussion.

Often a group of children will play happily in close proximity, so it's wise to avoid rules about how many children can play in an area.

High/Scope Curriculum. There are a number of reasons for this. First, it is often unclear what the ideal number of children is for each area. There are times when six or more children will manage well in the block area and times when two children have a very difficult time sharing the space and materials. Moreover, having two to three children share a single piece of equipment, such as a computer, can create a healthier, more interactive experience for children than having just one child use it. Second, knowing how to share space and materials is an essential life skill; it is important for adults to expect and embrace opportunities to help children problem-solve on these occasions. Children's solutions may include taking turns, but we should not mandate this. Third, and perhaps most important, limiting the number of children in areas encourages exclusion. In classrooms where such limits are used, children are often observed shouting commands like "Get out! You can't be in here — there are four children already!" Thus, limiting the numbers of children in areas often creates more problems than it solves.

•

Planning playful, supportive transitions between the components of the daily routine can make the difference between a day that flows easily and one that feels tense and out of control. When adults are aware that transitions can be challenging for children and find fun ways to support them as they move between activities, they will contribute to children's sense of success, competence, and self-esteem, as well as reduce the possibility of conflicts.

Top Tips for "Between Times" Transitions

- **Plan and maintain a consistent daily routine.** Children will be more comfortable moving between activities if they are familiar with the parts of the routine and the sequence they occur in every day.

- **Plan fun ways to move from one space or activity to another.** Transition activities should support children as active, whole-body learners.

- **Vary your transition strategies to keep them fresh.** Even the most interesting activity repeated too many times will become boring, and children's attention will be lost.

- **Post some favorite transition ideas,** placing them in transition areas, or write specific ideas on your team plan for the day.

- **Give a warning before the transition is about to happen and then signal its beginning.** Use verbal warnings, songs, special sounds, or other concrete experiences as signals.

- **Begin small- and large-group activities right away without waiting for the entire group to assemble.** When something interesting is happening, children will come and join quickly, wanting to be part of the fun.

- **Plan rest time in stages for a gradual slowdown.** Be prepared to spend time with children to help them settle in for a rest.

- **Set clear yet flexible expectations for rest time behavior.** Allow for individual differences in children's needs at this time.

- **Plan strategies and experiences for turn-taking situations.** Have props and strategies prepared so you are ready when the need for turns arises.

- **Use the six problem-solving steps** when conflicts arise over sharing of space or materials.

4

Waiting in Line = Wasted Time: Instead, Circle Up!

Expecting young children to wait with nothing to do is an invitation to chaos. Yet times in which children are expected to wait quietly and passively are common in many programs; these include waits for the beginning of large-group time, hand washing, toothbrushing, toileting, lunch preparation, and any occasion when everyone is leaving the classroom. Children are typically asked to stand in lines as many as three to six times a day — and all of this is unproductive and sets children up to fail.

Lining Up — Why Alternatives Are Needed

Teachers and caregivers often will tell you that they ask children to line up for a number of reasons. Some say this is the most orderly way to wait for a turn at the sink or to leave the room; others say that the line-up makes it clear who is first to do something; still others maintain that children need to "learn to line up" because they will have to in kindergarten. Line-ups in the early childhood classroom have been used for a long time, especially in full-day programs; they are a tradition that is now recognized by many as developmentally *inappropriate*. Children may indeed be required to line up when they are in elementary school; however, this skill will be most easily learned when it is easier developmentally. It is useful to keep in mind that even adults do not like to wait in line, but in an early childhood classroom, where learning is the main priority, waiting in lines not only is unpleasant and frequently leads to conflict but also is wasteful of learning time.

Plan ways to avoid mealtime waits. Here, as helpers set the table, the rest of the children participate in a number activity and leave one by one for the table.

Children are active learners who learn best by using materials, moving their hands or their whole bodies, making choices, singing, or talking. They can be learning all the time, as long as they are active with their minds or bodies. Understanding children's need to be active, adults planning routines for children should try to avoid waiting time altogether. If waiting is absolutely necessary, however, teachers and caregivers can enrich these times with activities that engage children's energy and continue the learning process. This kind of support leads to increased cooperation and collaboration among children, easing the transition for everyone.

Let's look more closely at what adults are trying to accomplish with line-ups and consider how this time might be used instead to maximize learning and accomplish the tasks at hand.

Ideas for Active Wait Times

Guidelines for planning

Below are some general guidelines for making your wait times more active, followed by some activity ideas that work well at these times.

✔ *Plan ways to avoid waiting times altogether.*

Reconsider all waiting periods. Many waits that are a standard part of the routine in some preschools, such as for toileting and hand washing, can be avoided with a bit of planning. It is especially important to avoid having children wait while sitting in front of food.

✔ If waiting can't be avoided, consider "circling up" rather than lining up.

Waiting in any grouping is difficult for children but asking young children to wait *in line* invites special difficulties. A primary developmental characteristic of young children is egocentricity (self-centeredness) — they have difficulty seeing things from the other person's point of view and tend to put themselves first. Since only one person *can* be first in a line, it's easy to understand why lines are such a challenge. The children in the middle often do not have enough physical space around them to avoid even accidental touching and pushing, and the child who is last is in the position that no one seems to like.

So why have lines? Why not have children wait in a circle with the supporting adult? While children are preparing to wash hands or use the toilet, they can participate in an active circle activity. To get started, call out "Circle up" and begin something fun. Circles avoid all the line difficulties described above, plus they make it possible for children to engage in experiences that are active and even educational.

Circling up is both a strategy and an activity. Teachers and caregivers will find that once they grasp the concept of gathering children in an active circle, rather than a passive line-up, they can use this strategy as they prepare to leave the classroom or playground, as they support bathroom turns, and on other occasions. The circle-up formation is a flexible grouping that adapts to the situation. After a group time, for example, the group may form a circle and begin a simple activity. The circle uncoils as it moves to the sink or door, then forms again, with the activity continuing until the next part of the routine begins. The circle-up provides a way to flow seamlessly from place to place. Circle-up activities are highly adaptable and have many variations, from songs to riddles to fingerplays and more. They can be planned ahead of time or done spontaneously as the need arises. Circling up creates fun and learning during transitions that might otherwise be chaotic and disconnected.

If possible, provide a space for circling up by making a circle on the floor near the sink or other waiting place, using letters, shapes, animals, numbers, and so forth to mark the spaces for children. As children are

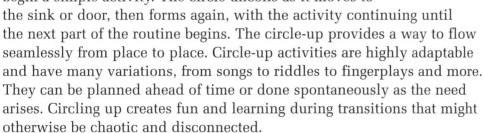

As children finish a circle activity, a child leads the group out the door and down the hall to the bathroom. The circle unwinds and children follow happily — no need for waiting in a line!

Instead of lining up to wait and wasting learning time...

...consider having children circle up for games, songs, and movement activities. Children learn while they wait and have fun!

coming over to the circle, ask them to stand on one of the pictures or symbols. Begin a game, fingerplay, or song for them to join as they are arriving (such as "Slippery Hands," described on p. 78 for hand washing). Each round of the activity ends with a child leaving to take a turn at the sink, toilet, and so forth.

✔ *Plan active experiences for all wait periods.*

Do not expect children to wait with nothing to do for any length of time. Write your plans for wait times on your regular daily plan. Be ready to spontaneously initiate ideas as well. Once a wait time has begun, you can also ask children who are waiting for activity ideas.

✔ *Post a list of "active waiting" ideas in the areas where children typically wait.*

Possible places include the sink, the door, the entrance or exit to the gross-motor area, or a space by the lunch table. Put together a box of simple things children can hold or manipulate while they are waiting, and keep it near the waiting areas.

✔ *Take a problem-solving approach if difficulties arise when children are waiting or moving in lines.*

Be prepared to acknowledge children's feelings of impatience. "You're really having a hard time waiting. This seems slow and boring, so let's do something fun!" Be prepared to do "shorthand problem solving" (see p. 71) to mediate any disputes that arise during these times. If a major conflict erupts and there is not time to thoroughly resolve the issue, tell the children when you will problem-solve with them and then give two choices of what to do for now.

When something fun is happening by the door, children come quickly to "circle up," without any of the conflicts created by lining up.

Below are ideas for waiting-time games and strategies that make these times fun and educational. Some of these are general "circle-up" ideas that may be used or adapted for various transitions. Others are suitable for particular situations or locations.

General "circle-up" games and experiences

I spy — recognizing beginning sounds of words. Develop children's awareness of beginning sounds like /t/, /p/, and /tr/. Say, "I spy with my little eye something that begins with the /t/ sound — what could it be?" (table), "I spy with my little eye someone who's name starts with the /sh/ sound" (Shana), and so forth.

I spy — recognizing colors. Sing "I spy with my little eye something that is red" (a red ball), and so forth.

"Shorthand" Problem Solving for Waiting Times or Circle-up Time

Often, small disputes arise when children are waiting for or are on the way to the next activity when there is not enough time for a full problem-solving discussion. In these cases you will need to do a shortened version of the six-step problem-solving process normally used to resolve disputes in High/Scope programs (see Evans, 2002), letting children know when you will discuss the problem again. Here are two examples:

Example 1: Two children having a dispute on the stairs

1. **Stay calm.** Use a calm tone of voice and gentle body language to de-escalate the conflict.

2. **Name children's feelings.** "You're both really upset."

3. **Describe the problem you've observed.** "It looks like there's a problem with pushing (hitting, name-calling)."

4. **Restate the problem.** "You're having a problem with pushing (hitting, name-calling), *and* we have to keep moving down the stairs." (See explanation of the importance of the "and" on p. 92.)

5. **Give limited choices.** "We will problem-solve when we are outside [or whenever you will have more time]. But for now, Juan, your choices are that you can hold this hand or walk in front of me, and Tina, you can hold my other hand or walk behind me. Which will you do?" If they do not choose, tell them gently, "Choose quickly or I will need to choose for you. I think you will feel better if you choose yourself."

6. **Give follow-up support.** Problem-solve with them later, as promised, so that the underlying issue behind the problem is resolved and does not reoccur.

Example 2: A child who does not want to leave the playground

1. **Stay calm.** Use a calm tone of voice and gentle body language.

2. **Name the child's feelings.** "I know it's really hard to leave the playground. You've been having a really good time." (Pause, and give the child time to absorb that you really understand.)

3. **Describe the problem you've observed.** "We have a problem. You don't want to come inside."

4. **Restate the problem.** "You don't want to come inside, *and* everyone else is going in."

5. **Give limited choices.** "Your choices now are to hold my hand while we go inside or race me to the gate. Which would you like to do? I think if you choose you will feel better."

6. **Give follow-up support.** (Inside) "It was really hard for you to come inside today. What was happening?" Listen to the child, repeating back what he or she says. "It's lots of fun to be outside, isn't it? It's really important to come to the gate when it's time to go in. We go together so that everyone stays safe. What would make it easier for you to leave the playground?" (The child may or may not have ideas — mostly it's important that you try to involve him or her in trying to make this transition easier.) "You want more time outside? Okay, let's see if we can do that tomorrow." Follow up the next day by saying, if possible, that you are adding 5 or 10 minutes to outside time.

"I spy, with my little eye, something that is…"

The *"Put Your Hands On"* song works in a variety of circle-up situations.

"I spy" variation. Ask one child to use a paper towel tube to look at something while everyone else guesses what he or she is looking at. The child passes it on to the next child after the correct guess. Each child takes two or more turns until it is time for him or her to use the sink or toilet, leave for the gym, etc.

Making up riddles. Create riddles with the beginning sounds of words while you wait. For example, "It begins with the /b/ sound and you put it in the toaster"; "It begins with /n/ and you use it for smelling things." Once children get the idea, ask them to create the riddle.

Riddle variation. Make up riddles that encourage children to think about how they might solve social problems: "If you want a toy that someone else is using, you could say_____." (Sample answer: "Can I have a turn with that, please?") Or, "If you see someone grab a toy from someone else, you could say_____." (Sample answer: "We have a problem. You both want to play with this. Let's ask the teacher to help.")

Theme song. Sing a peppy song the children all know well and are enthusiastic about, such as the Sesame Street theme, "The Alphabet Song," "Jingle Bells," "Twinkle, Twinkle, Little Star," or old Beatles songs.

Theme song variations. Sing the theme song "down low," or "up high" (crouching down or stretching up); sing it softly, loudly, while marching or tiptoeing, and so forth. Ask the children to think of new movements to try to keep the song fresh.

"Put Your Hands On" song. Here is another song that works well for circling up:

(To the tune of "When You're Happy and You Know It")
Put your hands on your head, on your head,
Put your hands on your head, on your head,
Put your hands on your head, now pretend you're being
      fed,
Put your hands on your head, on your head.

Put your hands on your eyes, on your eyes,
Put your hands on your eyes, on your eyes,
Put your hands on your eyes, now pretend to wave good-
      bye,
Put your hands on your eyes, on your eyes.

Put your hands on your nose, on your nose,
Put your hands on your nose, on your nose,
Put your hands on your nose, now tiptoe upon your toes,
Put your hands on your nose, on your nose.

Put your hands on your lips, on your lips,
Put your hands on your lips, on your lips,
Put your hands on your lips, now pretend you're taking
      sips,
Put your hands on your lips, on your lips.

Put your hands on your shoulder, on your shoulder,
Put your hands on your shoulder, on your shoulder,
Put your hands on your shoulder, now pretend to lift a
      boulder,
Put your hands on your shoulder, on your shoulder.

Put your hands on your knees, on your knees,
Put your hands on your knees, on your knees,
Put your hands on your knees, now everybody say "Cheese!"
Put your hands on your knees, on your knees.

Put your hands on your toes, on your toes,
Put your hands on your toes, on your toes,
Put your hands on your toes, never, never, pick your nose
      — eeww…(or "ick")
Put your hands on your toes, on your toes.

Make up your own variations using children's suggestions.

Pass the bear. As children wait in a circle, pass a stuffed bear around the group. As you begin, say, "Bear, bear, here comes Bear. Your favorite ____ (ice cream, letter, holiday, food, etc.) he wants you to share." Give each child a turn to hold the bear and tell it about his or her favorite ice cream, letter, holiday, food, and so forth.

"Pass the bear" variations. Ask the children waiting for Bear to make a cradle with their arms so they are ready to hold Bear.

Fill-it-in rhyming. Use familiar lines from stories, songs, or nursery rhymes and encourage children to fill them in, for example: "I'll huff and I'll puff, and _____"; "One, two, buckle my _____"; "The eensy, weensy spider went up the _____"; "Fee, fie, fo, _____."

Guessing the parts of the daily routine. Hold up a photo of each part of the daily routine, and ask what comes next.

Attribute guessing game. "Guess what is furry and purrs?"; "Guess who has curly brown hair and is wearing red today?"

Story with magic words. Choose a "magic word"; then tell a story and have children signal when they hear the word. For example, say, "The magic word is *dinosaur*. When you hear the word *dinosaur* in the story, you can wave your hand. When you wave, I will say your name and you can go brush your teeth (get your coat/wash your hands)." Begin the story:

> *"Once upon a time long ago there were very large creatures roaming the earth. They had big teeth and long tails. Some of them ate leaves and some ate other animals. One very ferocious dinosaur was called Tyrannosaurus Rex...."*

Choose someone who is waving to go brush his or her teeth. Continue the story until all the children have left.

Magic word variations. Make the magic word a repeated word such as *honk-honk:* "The magic word is *honk-honk.* Not just one honk, but two together, *honk-honk."* Begin the story:

> *"Once there was a little red car. It wanted to be able to honk-honk like the other cars, but its horn would only make a tiny honk sound. One day a small child got into the little red car. The little red car was very happy. The child reached up and pressed on the horn and suddenly it made a honk-honk sound...."*

Or make the magic word a two-word phrase like *chocolate chip:* "The magic words are *chocolate chip,* not just chocolate or chip, but the two words together, *chocolate chip."* Begin the story:

> *"Once Mommy and I went to the store. I asked her if I could buy some chocolate. She said no, not today, but we can buy some potato chips. Then I asked her if I could buy a chocolate chip cookie and she said...."*

Pretend characters or animals. Ask children to pretend to be a character or an animal from a story that you've read (for example, a butterfly coming out of a cocoon) and act out what the character does while waiting in the circle.

---

*The magic word strategy and variations are adapted from *Fee, Fie, Phonemic Awareness: 130 Prereading Activities for Preschoolers* (p. 16), by Mary Hohmann, 2002, Ypsilanti, MI: High/Scope Press.

Lunchtime ideas

Many children are very hungry at mealtimes, and expecting them to wait with food in front of them is unrealistic (this is difficult even for hungry adults!). Involving two or three children in the setup of the meal is one way to keep children engaged. In addition, consider doing some of the following activities for children as the food is being set out and hand washing completed.

Songs at the table. If children must stay at the table, have everyone stand with their backs to their chairs, or turn the chairs out for sitting. Then lead children in a song, such as "Sitting in the Soup" or "Now's the Time" (see Chapter 3), or a fingerplay, such as "Eensy Weensy Spider."

Musical chairs. With chairs turned out, play music and ask children to move like animals, to walk sideways, or to count chairs together when walking around the table. Everyone sits down when the music stops (don't take a chair away as you would in the traditional game). This will keep children's hands, bodies, and minds occupied until it is time to eat.

Taking turns helping out engages children before meals and snacks. Here helpers bring utensils to the table (left), and carry in a crate of milk cartons (right).

As helpers finish setting up the table, the teacher plays a guessing game with the rest of the children.

Self-care turns: toothbrushing, washing hands, toileting

Busy hands. In some classrooms, children must go as a group to a bathroom down the hall. This can present special challenges as it may take 10–15 minutes for everyone to have a turn. Any of the "circle-up" ideas can work on these occasions. Also, in some classrooms where it is necessary to wait with six to eight children, adults can take small rug squares or other items for children to sit on. From these "bases" they can then use the following "busy hands" ideas:

Waiting in a circle, have similar small objects, clay, or play dough ready in a basket or bucket. Give each child something small to hold and play with: a small ball of clay or play dough; a cotton ball; a small car or animal; a short, slightly bent length of pipe cleaner; and so forth. Assign a "helper" (perhaps the last child in line) to collect these in the basket or bucket as children leave the circle to brush their teeth or go into the hall to the bathroom.

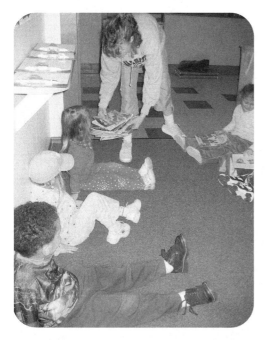

Children are given "salaman-der seats" as a base with their names and books to explore as they wait for a bathroom turn.

When the bathroom is outside the classroom, the teacher gives support by joining in the waiting activities.

Group toothbrushing. As an alternative to circling up at the bathroom, have children brush to music as a whole group, after a meal when they are already at the table. Any selection of music that has a peppy beat can make this fun. Special selections such as "Teeth Are Neat" and other songs from the *My Bodyworks: Songs About Your Bones, Muscles, Heart and More!* book with CD (Jane and Steven Schoenberg, 2005) work well. Ask children to brush until the music is finished. Provide a cup with a "sip" of water for each child so he or she can rinse and spit it back.

Toothbrushing turns. Ask four to five children at a time to circle up at the sink. Each child takes a turn at brushing as the group times him or her by singing a favorite song one or more times through. Use a song that can include the child's name, for example,

> (To the tune of "Happy Birthday")
> Happy toothbrushing to you,
> Happy toothbrushing to Jacob... (and so forth)

Musical hand washing. During a small-group circle-up by the sink, squirt a bit of soap in each child's hands as the group sings a favorite song. Sing the song for as long as it takes each child to wash. Songs with at least one verse and the possibility of using names (as in the "Happy Toothbrushing" example) work well during this time. Additional examples are the following:

(To the tune of "Bingo")

It's time, it's time to wash our hands,

And this is how we'll do it:

Wash, wash, wash, wash, wash
    (instead of B-I-N-G-O),

Wash, wash, wash, wash, wash,

Wash, wash, wash, wash, wash,

And that is how we'll do it.

(Repeat the above verse, this time counting to 15 instead of saying "wash.")

Children enjoy singing along with others as they wash hands and prepare for lunch.

(To the tune of "Row, Row, Row Your Boat")

Wash, wash, wash your hands,

Wash your hands so clean,

We can wash the dirt away,

We're the washing team!

Wash, wash, wash your hands,

We wash them for so long,

We wash and wash and wash and wash

To keep our bodies strong!

Try making up new words to other favorite tunes with the children. Write down the words to your new song and post them near the sink. Support clean hands and budding songwriters!

Marching to the sink. Use circle-up as an opportunity for children to practice alliteration, which helps them become aware of word sounds. Here are some examples:

(For a circle-up to go to the sink)

Gee golly garch,

Everybody march.

Gee golly gircle,

Let's make a circle.

Gee golly gosh,

(Child's name), it's time to wash.

(Another idea for a circle-up to go to the sink)

Zip zang zoo zap,

Let's all give a clap.

Zip zang zoo zunch,

Let's get ready for our lunch!

Zip zang zoo zed,

As they wait to wash their hands, children explore and describe the "feel" of a little bit of soap.

Wash your hands if you have red.

Zip zang zoo zeen,

Wash your hands if you have green.

(Continue until all children have washed their hands.)

Slippery hands. When children are waiting to wash their hands before lunch, circle up and put a small amount of soap in the hands of the children waiting; encourage them to notice and describe the feel of the soap in their hands, then sing:

(To the tune of "Mary Had a Little Lamb")

We all have a little soap, little soap, little soap,

We all have a little soap, to scrub our hands today.

And every time we rub and rub, rub and rub, rub and rub,

Every time we rub and rub, we wash the dirt away.

Waiting for the bus

Slippery hands variation. Put a small amount of baby lotion or powder in the children's hands, encouraging them to notice and describe how it feels and smells.

Winter variation. If children are waiting for the bus with mittens on, encourage the children to use their mittens as puppets, singing a favorite song to each other, such as "Where is Thumbkin?" (using the thumb and all the fingers together for "Where is family?").

Actively moving from room to room

In many programs it is necessary, for a variety of reasons, for children to leave the classroom. Adults need strategies for leaving the room without disruptions; some ideas follow. At the end of this section are some suggestions for those times when moving in a line is necessary for safety.

Obstacle. When children are waiting to leave the classroom, gross-motor room, or other room, put a slide, a tunnel, a hoop, a small set of stairs, or a soft toy to jump over in front of the door children will be exiting from. As children come to the door one by one to leave (for gym, for the bathroom, for hand washing), sing a song that gives you the length of delay you need. For example, the adult and the rest of the group snap fingers, clap, or pat their knees to the beat as they chant the following:

> **Group:** Hey little duckie by my side. (Child is next to slide, tunnel, hoop, stairs, or toy.) Where are you going?
>
> **Child:** Going for a ride.

(Child moves over, under, or through the "obstacle" and leaves the room. If more time is needed, adult pretends not to hear the child, says "What?" and starts the chant again.)

If even more time is needed, try this variation. Clap hands with everyone while one child is by your side and chant:

> **Adult:** Jingle, jingle, jangle, jen,
>
> Everyone clap and count to ten.
>
> **Group:** (Speaking slowly as the child moves over, under, or through the obstacle.) One, two, three…

Moving train or animals. When the children are leaving a gym or large-motor space, adult calls to children, "Let's be a train chugging around the room! All aboard — the train is leaving!" The children begin chugging as they follow the adult in a "train" line (or the line can be a hissing snake, a roaring dinosaur, and so forth). The adult walks quickly, then jogs, doing several laps until all the children have joined, then slows down and approaches the exit door. Children follow the adult out of the room. The second adult follows at the end of the line.

Olympic jogger variation. Call out, "Let's be Olympic joggers!" (Adult jogs in a circle.) Everyone follows the adult (or line leader). Jog several times around in a circle until everyone is jogging, then slow to a walk and go out the door.

Sign reading. Use child-made hand-held signs to signal GO or STOP as children arrive at the door to leave the classroom. The signs should use colors or sym-

"All aboard — the train is leaving!"

Sometimes lining up is necessary for safety. Instead of asking children in a line not to move, not to use their hands, and not to express themselves out loud...

...consider ways to move in lines so that children will be safe AND continue to learn. Ask children for their ideas for fun ways to move.

bols as well as lettering to help children decode the message easily. Once children understand how the signs work, you can ask them to take turns being the sign-holder.

Sign-reading variations. Use SLOW for walking down the hall and FAST for when you get to the playground; if you are truly daring, use QUIET for walking down the hall and LOUD when you get to the playground.

Magic fairy dust. As children leave to go in the hall, sprinkle them with "fairy dust" (glitter or baby powder) to make them "fly like a bird," "swim like a fish," "tiptoe like a spy," "slide like an ice skater," and so forth; or sprinkle it directly on their hands to hold and explore.

Fairy dust variations. Use a "wand" and touch each child as they move through the door or gate.

Blowing bubbles. As each child leaves, use a straw to blow a "bubble" around them. Say, "Take care not to touch anything as you float down the hall."

A safe alternative to walking in a line is to walk "octopus-style." Strings of children form the tentacles by holding hands with classmates and adults.

> ### Moving Children Along a Busy Street
>
> Joe and Maria need to move with their group of 15 children from the playground, down the sidewalk next to a busy street, and into the Head Start building. As they stand at the playground preparing to leave, they ask the children, "How would you like to move down the sidewalk today?" The children, remembering the butterflies they've just seen, respond, "Butterflies! Let's be butterflies!" Joe and Maria nod enthusiastically and they begin to move through the gate, with Maria in front and Joe following at the end. As they move along, Joe sees several children drifting to the edge of the sidewalk and suggests that they tickle the wall with their "wings." The children who have moved out to the edge of the sidewalk quickly move closer to the wall, sweeping their hands up and down the wall as they flutter their "wings." They all are now at a safe distance from the street and the transition continues smoothly into the building.

Go when it rhymes. Before leaving, say, "When you hear a word that rhymes with your name, go down the hall: Head, sky, nose, jam (Sam)."

Soft chicks. Give children a soft yarn "chick" (pompom) to carry safely to the "nest" as they walk down the hall. As they arrive, hold out the nest (a basket with Easter grass or shredded paper) so they can put in their chick.

Chicks variation. Instead of using pompoms for chicks, give children cotton balls or small balls of clay. Or give them "tickets" (small pieces of stiff paper) to carry that they can use to gain admission at the door to the room that is their destination.

Spontaneous rhymes for walking in a line. At those times when a line is absolutely necessary for safety, for example, when the group is moving down a hall, a staircase, or a sidewalk, the adult can chant or sing in a military style: "Walking feet are really neat." Children chant or sing back, "Walking feet are really neat! One, two, three, four, five, six, seven, eight, nine, ten" (said slowly, one number for each marching step). Then the adult chants, "Dancing hands are really grand." Children wiggle their fingers and repeat, "Dancing hands are really grand! One, two, three, four, five, six, seven, eight, nine, ten" while continuing to march along.

Rhyming variation. Instead of counting, ask children to say the alphabet, "Walking feet are really neat, A, B, C, D...."

• ➥

Teachers and caregivers in early childhood settings work hard to keep waiting time to a minimum, knowing that inactive time is very uncomfortable for children and critical learning time can be lost. Despite adults' best efforts to reduce the amount of waiting and line-up time, a certain amount of waiting may happen in some group settings. When teachers plan active experiences for these times, using creative strategies to support children as they move from one space to another, they can make very effective use of these occasions. These experiences help children learn to function cooperatively in groups while enabling the group to accomplish necessary tasks. When teachers and caregivers facilitate fun and learning during these transitions, children become more skilled at managing transitions in general, skills they will use throughout their lives.

Top Tips for Waiting Times

- **Avoid having children wait.** Reconsider all waiting periods. It is especially important to avoid having children wait while sitting in front of food.

- **If waiting can't be avoided, consider "circling up" rather than lining up.** While children are preparing to wash their hands or use the toilet, they can participate in an active circle activity. If the turn-taking is lengthy, pass out mats, sit down on them, and use small materials together.

- **Plan active experiences for all wait periods.** Do not expect children to wait with nothing to do for any length of time. Write your plans for wait times on your regular daily plan.

- **Post a list of active waiting ideas in the areas where children typically wait.** Include a list of your favorite songs or riddles. Put together a box of simple things children can hold or manipulate while they are waiting, and keep it near the waiting areas.

- **Take a problem-solving approach to wait-time difficulties.** If children are frustrated about having to wait, acknowledge their feelings of impatience, and give them something active to do. Be prepared to do "shorthand problem solving" to mediate any disputes that arise, and be sure to return to the discussion later when there is more time.

5
Cleanup Time —
More Than a Transition

Cleanup time is often a hectic part of the day that is carried out in haste as everyone focuses on what will happen after the cleanup is finished. And because cleanup is usually considered to be a transition time, rather than a component of the daily routine, it is often given little thought during planning. This approach can cause problems for children and classroom adults. If teachers and caregivers do not plan ways to support children during this period and if there is not enough time allotted to make cleanup work successfully, difficulties and conflicts may arise. Many teachers expect that cleanup will simply "happen"; however, this is rarely the case.

Cleanup: Part of the Educational Routine

This chapter suggests a different approach. Rather than thinking of cleanup only as a transition time, we encourage teachers and caregivers to include cleanup as a full-fledged daily routine component and plan for it accordingly. Just as they make daily plans for large-group time, small-group time, and other important activities, adults need to plan daily cleanup strategies and experiences that will support children in enjoying this activity and learning from it. Included here are many suggestions that will transform cleanup time into an important and educational part of the daily routine.

When creating any daily routine component for young children, it is important to re-member that each time period is part of the educational and social structure of the day — even cleanup time. In fact, this particular part of the day provides special opportunities for building a *sense of community* and *shared control and responsibility*. As children put materials away as a team, adults can encourage activities that become rich social learning experiences.

During cleanup time adults can create a wide variety of opportunities for learning. Consider all the abilities that are developing as children clean up; the following are some possibilities. As children put things away on labeled shelves, they are classifying objects by attributes such as size, shape, color, and function. As they put away objects in their assigned spaces, they are noticing relationships such as length, thickness, position, and quantity. For example, they see that objects are seriated (ordered by size) when they put small, medium, and large pots away on a shelf marked with small, medium, and large outlines indicating where the pots go. They are considering concepts of number when they notice that there are three kinds of paintbrushes, each with its own container, and when they see that each marker corresponds to one hole on the marker holder. As they put away art materials, they may be sorting by color. As they work with other children, they are experiencing collaboration and developing an understanding of the outcomes of collective community work. As they take care of their space, they will understand the cause-and-effect connection between taking responsibility for cleanup and having a well-organized room where toys and materials are easy to find. Ultimately, as children begin to enjoy cleanup, they will learn to respect the materials and the areas that have been provided for them.*

Cleanup is an opportunity for children to work cooperatively.

Children and Adults: Different Perspectives on Cleaning Up

Many teachers say that cleanup time is one of the most stressful parts of their day with children. When adults indicate that it is time to clean up, some children suddenly develop aches and pains, have pressing business at their cubbies, or simply disappear. Even children whom adults single out for special reminders often ignore requests to clean up. What are these children thinking? Why does cleanup time seem to be so difficult for young children?

To gain a better understanding of these issues, it helps to take a look at adults' typical expectations for this time of day. Teachers and caregivers often see cleanup as a time to regroup and gain a sense of order before moving on to the next part of the daily routine. Many teachers also feel they will be judged — by administrators, directors, or parents — on their classroom's neatness or on whether they have kept to the time allotted for each part of the day's schedule. As a result, teachers feel stressed.

---

*Several sections of this chapter have been adapted from articles by High/Scope early childhood specialist and demonstration preschool teacher Suzanne Gainsley (see Gainsley, 2005a, 2005b).

Children become very involved in their explorations — they don't worry about "making a mess."

If they can't get their children to clean up, what control do they have?

But is neatness actually related to teacher competence? A classroom filled with children initiating their own plans and engaged with materials will look "used." In fact, in a classroom where the children have been engaged in active learning, one would expect to find paint dripped on the floor, children moving materials from area to area, and children using lots of "stuff." Similarly, minor variations in time allotments indicate that teachers are considering children's engagement and interest as they move through the sequence of the day's activities, rather than imposing a rigid and unresponsive schedule.

To rethink your adult expectations for children at this time, try looking at cleanup from the child's viewpoint. Young children live in the moment. If we ask them to think about the cleanup consequences of dumping out all the beads in a box in order to find the purple ones, or of packing all the baby diapers, bottles, dishes, and clothes into the shopping bag for the "trip to Grandma's house," they will usually brush this off with the automatic response, "We know. We'll clean it up." Their current plans and interests are the priority — not future needs for order. Remember, too, that being in control is a major motivational factor for preschoolers. In High/Scope settings, cleanup time occurs after a very active work time, where children initiate and carry out their plans and use materials in all kinds of ways. Children have been in control. But at cleanup time, it can feel to them that the control has been taken away.

Children's resistance to cleanup, then, is a natural result of their preference for the present over the future, their desire to carry out their plans and choices, and their need for control over their activities.

When adults observe carefully and acknowledge the importance of children's work, children are more willing to clean up.

Adopting a Positive Attitude

Understanding the perspective of children may not solve the problem of getting them to clean up, but it does help teachers and caregivers stay calm and approach cleanup more positively. Your own attitude is the key. Is cleanup something you dread? Try not to show it. Children will absorb and reflect those feelings. Nobody likes to do horrible chores! If you approach cleanup as just another interesting and possibly fun part of the daily routine, something people just do, many children will imitate your accepting, matter-of-fact attitude.

Getting down on children's level and explaining what will happen at cleanup in a positive and excited way encourages children to join in.

Your understanding of children's point of view and your positive attitude will reduce tensions and conflicts over cleanup. Many problems arise when adults have the unrealistic expectation that children will simply clean up their toys when they are told to do so. When children don't respond, adults may mistake this for "not listening," when in fact children are simply very excited about their play. If children express their dislike of cleaning, adults may consider this to be "talking back." This situation can easily escalate into a major confrontation with the adult ending up doing most of the cleanup, and the children feeling like they've been "bad." As illustrated in the drawings on pp. 90–91, the positive strategies described in this chapter can prevent such difficulties and turn cleanup into a "win-win" experience for all.

When children are supported with a cleanup warning and strategies that make cleanup time predictable and fun, they are motivated to participate in cleanup activities. These activities can be games, songs, and movement experiences that help create new skills and new learning.

Instead of expecting children to clean up on demand, create a cleanup time that is a predictable and fun component of the daily routine. When it's fun, children will clean up *with enthusiasm!*

Cleanup Strategies and Activities

General guidelines

After adopting a positive attitude, consider the following additional strategies to help children ease into this very busy part of the day.

✔ *Since young children yearn to do things independently and also like to do things they can be successful at, organize cleanup to promote children's independence and developing skills.*

If you haven't done this already, organize your classroom so that toys are stored on low shelves (rather than in closets or out of children's reach), so children can find and return materials themselves. Adding labels to shelves

Children will be successful at cleanup if the classroom is organized so they can find and put away materials themselves.

and containers helps children know where each item belongs. Keeping like materials together — all the unit blocks on the same shelf, the camping equipment next to the tent, and so on — helps children find and return materials.

✔ **Include cleanup time in your daily schedule, giving it a 10- to 15-minute time slot.**

Since treating cleanup as an important, thoughtfully considered part of the routine is essential to success, be sure you have allowed enough time for it. Providing a realistic amount of time for cleanup will help everyone to relax and enjoy it.

Adults and children put their hands in the air and chant, "Jingle, jungle, jangle, jean — Five more minutes and we will clean!"

✔ **Plan a cleanup strategy for each day (a game, song, or other playful experience), and write it down on your team's daily plan.**

This effort to plan ahead will keep cleanup time as fresh and exciting as other parts of the day. Your cleanup strategies should be active and varied. Strategies can incorporate symbols, songs, pretending, purposeful movement — anything that makes the experience fun and educationally worthwhile for children. Use a wide variety of strategies, changing them regularly (see examples in the following sections).

✔ **Plan ways to warn children that cleanup time is near.**

As you set cleanup time in motion, remember that children are involved in carrying out their plans and will need support in winding up their activities. Let children know that cleanup is coming up soon by giving them a five-minute warning (two two-minute warnings, or a five-minute and a one-minute warning). There are many ways to communicate this: simply make an announcement; whisper a secret message from ear to ear around the classroom; or get children's attention by shaking a tambourine, turning a rain stick, or ringing a bell. In some classrooms, children participate in giving the warning signal. For example, a child can hold up a card with a large number and say, "Five minutes (or one or two minutes) until cleanup." As the warning is announced, tell the children what the cleanup strategy of the day will be: "Five more minutes to cleanup, and today we'll be doing a parade cleanup!" Then, a few minutes later, use a second signal (such as playing an instrument, turning the lights on and off, or simply beginning the activity) to indicate that it is now time to clean up. It is okay to begin the cleanup strategy for the day without waiting until all children are ready. They are more likely to join in if they see that other children are already having fun.

Visual warning signals can be important for children with hearing impairments. For example, a child can turn the lights off and on to signal the beginning of cleanup or hold up a sign with a large numeral 1 to indicate that cleanup will begin in one minute.

Instead of expecting children to clean up on demand...

...create a cleanup time that is a predictable and fun component of the daily routine. Support children with games, songs, and movement experiences that help create new skills and new learning. When it's fun, children will clean up with enthusiasm!

✔ **Save works-in-progress.**

Though you may have alerted them to the end of work time, children often have finishing touches to add to their work. Some children may have spent their entire work time preparing materials to use in pretend play. For example, they may have made a cake, written invitations, and wrapped presents for a birthday party but have no time left to actually pretend to have the party. In some classrooms, children use "work-in-progress" signs to save unfinished work. These are premade signs that are laid over the materials to be saved.

Signs warn others not to touch children's work so they can return to it at another time.

When children understand that they will be able to return to their materials later or the next day, they are more willing to stop working for a time. But even after all the warnings, some children still resist. Sometimes, just acknowledging children's interests and feelings — for example, saying, "I know you don't want to stop now. You're really having fun with the baby, and you can make a plan to play with the baby tomorrow" — will help children let go of their resistance.

✔ **Break down large cleanup tasks into smaller jobs.**

Sometimes just looking at the pile of toys on the floor can be enough to tire out both teachers and children — so find ways to divide up big jobs. For example, in one preschool, when three children made a large mixed pile of Legos, shells, and pegs, a teacher passed out small plastic cups to the three and suggested that each child fill the cup with one of the materials needing to be sorted. The teacher also joined in to help. See also "Stepping stones" (p. 96) and "Bucket brigade" (p. 97) for more ideas for putting away large amounts of materials.

✔ **Use group discussion when cleanup fizzles.**

There are always days when it seems everyone is playing instead of cleaning up and children don't respond to your reminders or the fun activities you have planned. At these times, one strategy that can be helpful is to stop and regroup with a class dis-

---

How "And" Smooths the Way

It can be challenging to make positive and encouraging statements that acknowledge what children are feeling *and* what adults want children to do next. The challenge is to value equally the feelings and needs of the adult and child. When we want children to do what *we* want, it is important to begin a dialogue that encourages the child to want to listen to us. Rather than being directive and telling children "Look at me. Listen to me," try to sincerely acknowledge what they are doing and the fun they are having: "You're so excited about the new fire trucks." After doing this, avoid continuing with your needs by saying "But...." This will negate your acknowledging, understanding statement about the child's interests. Instead, say, "*And* the trucks need to be put away so we can go out." This simple language change can make a big difference for children, eliciting greater cooperation *and* more listening.

To make this big cleanup job less overwhelming, the teacher has suggested that each child fill up a small container with Legos.

cussion. The discussion is a problem-solving session, not a scolding. Following the discussion, children usually return to cleaning up with renewed energy and purpose. (For more on how these discussions work, see "When Cleanup Is Stalled, Try a Group Problem-Solving Discussion" on p. 94.)

✔ *Structure your cleanup time as a "community" cleanup.*

This means allowing children to choose to clean in areas of the room *other than* those they played in. As a result, children may not necessarily put away materials that they have personally used. Contrary to what some adults may expect, children are often more willing to put away materials they have not played with, especially if they have spent a long time playing in a different area.

✔ *As you work, strive to set aside adult notions of tidiness.*

Expect the environment to be cleaned to children's standards. Children are more likely to experience success if adults have reasonable expectations. This may mean that some items are left out.

To sum up, at cleanup time, encourage children's intrinsic motivation for the task by creating an

In a "community cleanup," everyone works together to clean the whole classroom, and children do not always clean the area where they played.

When Cleanup Is Stalled, Try a Group Problem-Solving Discussion

Have you ever had a cleanup time when hardly anybody seems to be cleaning up and nothing you can say to children seems to help? At these times, one strategy we use in our classroom is to stop and regroup with a class discussion.

The children know that when we have a problem to solve, we gather on the blue rug in the block area. Teachers may be tempted to begin the discussion by praising those children who were cleaning up — for example, "I like the way Justin put away all the trains." This singles out some children and may make them or the others feel anxious or resentful, however. If adults blame children and threaten them with punitive consequences, then the excuses start: little voices saying "But I was cleaning," and little fingers pointing, accusing others of playing or goofing around. A more positive strategy is for adults to calmly describe how they are feeling (using "I" statements, not "you" statements); for example, "I'm frustrated that the block area is still messy" or "I feel like I am doing most of the work myself." Rather than focus on the negative, adults can also pose the question "How are we going to get this room ready for recall?" There are always plenty of children who respond, "Let's clean up!" It is also helpful to remind the children that there are consequences of not cleaning up (natural consequences, not punishments). Play dough that gets left out and dries overnight is a natural consequence. (As a science experiment, try letting it sit out one night.) An extra-long cleanup time, which takes time away from the other, more enjoyable parts of the day, is another natural consequence.

During one group discussion we asked the children, "Why should we clean up?" Here are some of their responses:

> "Because it's really messy. If we just left it messy, it would be very messy all the time. People would trip on stuff."

> "The visitors would trip."

> "If I were trying to make a ship or something, I would have to find something else [to use]. There wouldn't be enough stuff [available on the shelf]."

> "All the paint would be on the floor."

> "That would be slippery."

Then we asked, "Why is cleanup time so hard?" Children replied, "It's work" and "No fun." One child said it best: "We like playing more than cleaning up." We then asked how we could make cleanup more fun. Many children remembered how we occasionally play cleanup games. Irene suggested we play red light, green light, a game in which children put things away when the caller says "Green light" and stop when the caller says "Red light."

After children have made their suggestions, we usually ask children to make a cleanup plan. We may ask each child to stand in the area he or she will clean up, or we may ask each child to hold up the first thing he or she will put away. This gives children a starting point. After one cleanup discussion, I asked a child to go to the house area and give us a report on its condition. His response was, "Stuff's on the floor under the table. There's water spilled." I then asked, "How many helpers do you think it will take to clean up the house area?" We then asked for volunteers to start in each area. At times like this, it may seem fairer to expect those who played in specific areas to help clean up those spaces; yet often it is other children who will volunteer. We go with their plan, since this gives the children a sense of control.

After the discussion and reorganization, cleanup usually continues at a much more productive pace. Teachers then offer the group encouragement, such as "Wow, this room is looking cleaner!" or "Look how fast we can do it when we all work together."

— From "Cleanup Time: What Are Those Children Thinking?" by Suzanne Gainsley in *Supporting Young Learners 4: Ideas for Child Care Providers and Teachers* (N.A. Brickman, H. Barton, & J. Burd, Eds.), 2005b, Ypsilanti, MI: High/Scope Press, p. 88.

experience that is interesting and enjoyable, provides choices, and enables children to be successful. In other words, provide an experience that children will look forward to participating in every day.

Cleanup-time strategies and experiences

The following ideas and strategies are designed to add playfulness to cleanup time, motivating young children to participate happily. The memory of cleanup as another fun part of the day will help in subsequent days, since children are usually asked more than once a day to put materials away. This playful approach will likely increase the overall level of cooperation and adult-child partnership as everyone takes care of the classroom space. Each of the ideas and strategies described below assumes that adults have embraced the notion of a *community* cleanup.

Cleanup Clown's colors. Show a large picture of "Cleanup Clown" (a clown drawn with primary colors with different colors for the hat, hair, nose, shirt, bow tie, pants, shoes, etc.). Start with the hat, showing the children and saying, "Can anyone find something the same color as Cleanup Clown's *(name of color)* hat to put away?" When the children are finished with that color, move to another part of the room as you show children the next color, continuing like this until cleanup is complete.

Mystery symbols. If you haven't done this already, make signs for each of the classroom interest areas (art area, block area, computer area, toy area, book area, and so forth). Each sign should have the area name, with the first letter in bold print, and a symbol, such as a simple drawing of two stacked blocks for the block area. It is important to keep the symbols easy to draw so that children can try to reproduce them. Make cards or "tickets" that have the area symbols on them, laminate them, and place them in a basket. Ask each child to choose a ticket from the basket, match it with the area sign, and then go to clean up in that area.

Mystery symbols variations. Instead of having children draw from a basket, hold up a "ticket" with an area symbol, and let children choose the area they want to clean. Later in the year, put a large letter that is the first letter of the area's name on the ticket. Have several other such tickets ready for each of the areas that need cleaning so that there will be one ticket for

"Who has something to put away that is the same color as Cleanup Clown's hair?"

Cleanup "tickets" for the play areas can be used for many cleanup games.

each child that chooses to go to that area. Ask "What symbol (or letter) is this?" As children answer, hand them the ticket they identified and ask them to find the symbol or letter on an area sign and go to that area to clean up. Give extra support to any children who seem confused by the letters.

Draw your own area symbol. If children are very familiar with the area symbols, give them an index card and ask them to draw or write on it the symbol, first letter, or entire word for the area where they would like to clean up. Ask them to give you the card or put it in a special box or pocket.

Mystery letters variation. As children get to know the first letters for the area names and show interest in the whole words, provide tickets with the entire word for the area, without the symbol.

Giant cleanup. When you give the five-minute cleanup warning, tell children, "In five minutes you will hear a giant's voice saying 'Fee, Fie, Fo, Fean.' Listen carefully, and see if you can hear how many things you should clean up today." When five minutes has passed, chant in a deep "giant's voice": "Fee, Fie, Fo, Fean. Today we'll find *six* things to clean." Repeat until everyone is cleaning. If just a bit more cleaning is needed, sing again, "Fee, Fie, Fo, Fean. Now find two more things to clean," and so on.

"Quick, put them in — I hear the giant coming!"

Giant cleanup variation. Use another favorite voice you have used in a story, for example, the Big Bad Wolf from "Three Little Pigs" or Baby Bear from "Goldilocks and the Three Bears."

Stepping stones. If children have moved a lot of materials from one area to another, lay down two lines of "stepping stones" (mats) for moving to and from the area with the materials.

Bucket cleanup. This strategy is one way to make big cleanup jobs less overwhelming by breaking down the task. This encourages children to see cleanup as a series of smaller, doable jobs that can be completed one at a time. Give children small plastic "cleanup buckets" with handles (paint buckets that can be purchased inexpensively at a hardware or paint store work well for this). The children collect materials in their buckets, put the items away, then refill their buckets for another small job. Some children fill their buckets to the brim with materials, and others use them to carry one toy at a time. Each time they empty their bucket, children experience a small success.

Bucket variation. Add an exciting twist to this activity by handing children cleanup buckets that teachers have already filled with "mystery toys" to put away.

Bucket brigade (with or without buckets). Have a group of children form a line from one area of the room to another, and pass toys down the line, with the last child putting the toy on the shelf. This worked well in one classroom as children passed dirty dishes from the table in the house area across the room to the sink to be washed.

A rack for drying paintings allows children to put away their own work.

Miss Mary Mack. As children begin to clean, sing this familiar song:

> Miss Mary Mack, Mack, Mack,
>
> The toys go back, back, back,
>
> 'Til the room is done, done, done,
>
> Cleanup is fun, fun, fun.

Encourage the children to sing with you.

Miss Mary Mack variation. Ask several children to be the "Miss Mary Mack Choir." Ask them to move around the room singing the tune, providing musical support as children clean.

Happy cleanup. To the tune of "Happy Birthday," sing "Happy cleanup today," repeating this four times. As a variation try "Happy feet today" or "Happy hands today."

Tickle me! Using a feather duster, a feather, or some other soft object, move around the room and "dust" the children who are cleaning. Sing:

> (To the tune of "Frère Jacques")
>
> Who is cleaning? Who is cleaning?
>
> Here I come, here I come,
>
> Dust, dust, dust, dust,
>
> Dust, dust, dust, dust,
>
> I'll dust (child's name),
>
> I'll dust (same child or another child).

Repeat the song throughout the cleanup. *Note:* Take care not to dust children who do not want to be dusted.

Clickety-clack, clickety-clack. Pass out bags (either large paper grocery bags with handles or gift bags) for children to fill with materials they are putting away. As children clean, sing the following song (add sound effects by snapping your fingers or clapping):

(To the tune of "The Adams Family"/"Days of the Week" song)

Clickity-clack (snap, snap), clickity-clack (snap, snap),

Put things back, in the sack, clickety-clack (snap, snap),

Clickity-clack (snap, snap), clickity-clack, (snap, snap),

Put things back, in the sack, clickety-clack (snap, snap).

After the children have collected some items, chant:

Clickity-clay (snap, snap), clickity-clay (snap, snap),

Put them away, put them away, put them away (snap, snap),

Clickity-clay (snap, snap), clickity-clay (snap, snap),

Put them away, put them away, put them away (snap, snap).

Encourage children to chant with you.

More alliteration chants. Make up cleanup chants based on familiar rhymes and chants with alliterations, such as "Peter, Peter Pumpkin-eater," "Snip, Snap, Snrrr," and "Hippity-hop, hippity-hop." One easy alliteration game is to begin an action (clapping, tapping shoulders, and so forth) and say to the beat of the action, "Jingle, jingle, jangle, jouse — all the bears (or tigers/mice/dogs, etc.) clean the house." Then chant, "Jingle, jingle, jangle, jocks — all the horses clean the blocks," and so forth. (See Hohmann, 2002, Chapter 3, for more ideas.)

Robot man. Using a robot voice and movements, move around the room pointing to objects and speaking to children:

Robot man sees a ____, please put ____ on the shelf.

Robot man sees a ____, please put ____ in the bin.

(Continue with other objects that need to be cleaned up.)

If you're happy, yahoo. Begin by clapping your hands or shaking an instrument. Then begin to sing this song:

(To the tune of "If You're Happy and You Know It")

If you're happy and you know it, find a toy,

If you're happy and you know it, find a toy,

If you're happy and you know it, and you really want to show it,

If you're happy and you know it, find a toy.

If you're happy and you know it, find its place,

If you're happy and you know it, find its place,

If you're happy and you know it, and you really want to show it,

If you're happy and you know it, find its place.

If you cleaned up and you know it, give a shout, yahoooo!

If you cleaned up and you know it, give a shout, yahoooo!

If you cleaned up and you know it, and you really want to show it,

If you cleaned up and you know it, give a shout, yahoooo!

Repeat until the room is clean.

Yahoo variation. In the last verse, after singing "If you cleaned up and you know it," sing "Jump in place," "Shake a hand," or "Give a wave" instead of "Yahoo," and do this as you sing.

Marching to music. Put on marching music and march around the room. When the music stops, the children clean up wherever they have stopped. After two to three minutes, begin the music again and encourage the children to march again. Stop the music after a few minutes of marching, making sure to time it so that children are near messy areas. Repeat this sequence until the room is clean.

Music variations. Choose a different style of music for moving around the room: opera, a classic wedding march, or culturally diverse music like bagpipes (Scottish) or pan flutes (South American). Ask children to move however they would like to the music, then stop the music and have everyone clean. Or, give children bells or shaking instruments they have made. Put on a favorite piece of marching music and have everyone march around the room shaking the instruments until the music stops.

Monster man. Sing in a gruff voice:

(To the tune of "Row, Row, Row Your Boat")

Monster, monster, monster man,

Moving 'round the room.

Finding something to pick up,

Vroom, vroom, vroom.

Monster, monster, monster man,

Moving 'round the space.

Grrrrr, grrrrr, grrr, grrrr,

Cleaning up the place.

Encourage children to be "monster man," growling as they clean. Repeat until the room is clean.

Monster man variation. Cut out several large monster faces out of cardboard, leaving a large hole for the monster's mouth on each one. Have children draw or paint the details of the faces on the cardboard. At cleanup time, set up the faces (or hold them up) in front of or over the toy shelves or bins. Children then put the toys on the shelf or in the bin by "feeding" the monster. You can replace the monsters with dinosaurs or other animals that the children in your classroom are interested in.

Cleanup train. Have each adult gather together a small group of children and form a "train." Move around the room together, chugging and blowing your whistles, then stop at an interest area and have the whole

The "cleanup train" travels around the room, stopping to clean where needed.

"train" clean up that area. When all the toys are put away, reassemble the train and continue on to the next messy area.

Train variation. Instead of a train, the group can be a "hissing snake," a "toy-gobbling, eight-headed dragon," "extra smart puppies," or any other animal or animal grouping of current interest to the children.

Train variation with tickets. Use a roll of plain labels for tickets, putting colors, shapes, or other identifying features on the labels. If you have two adults, have two different sets of tickets, for example, red and yellow. Form trains according to which tickets children have, with an adult supporting the children in each train in putting away materials that match their "tickets."

Sticker graphing. Create a graph, using laminated poster board (for easy reuse) or a large piece of white paper. Put the area symbols at the top with columns underneath each symbol. Ask the children to look at each area and estimate how many people it will take to clean the area, then agree on the size of the teams. With the children, decide which teams will clean in each area. As the teams finish their work, give a sticker to each team member to put on the graph. The columns will then show the differences in the group sizes. Consider doing this several times in a row so the children can thoroughly experience and understand the number concepts involved and see which areas require more people to get them tidy.

Graph variation. Instead of using stickers, assign each team a marker color. Each team member will then put a mark of that color in the column when their area is finished. The mark could be a simple dot of color, or the first letter of their name, or their letter link.

I spy. Divide the group in half. Give the "spy" group paper towel tubes. The other group are the "winged monkeys" (or any other favorite animals or characters). Ask the "spies" to move around the room looking for toys out of place. When they see something out of place, they say, "I spy with my little eye ____," and a "winged monkey" swoops over and puts the item away. After about five minutes, switch the roles for the two groups. At another time, children may enjoy making wings and/or decorating paper towel tubes for this activity.

"I spy" variation. On another day, introduce the "I spy" game, this time asking the children what they would like to be, other than winged monkeys.

Trick the teacher. Right after the five-minute warning, one adult asks the children if they would like to "trick the teacher." Of course, the answer will be yes! The adult whispers to them that when they hear the two-minute warning, everyone should quietly start to clean up *before* the cleanup signal. At the signal, the children begin to clean up, and the second adult goes to the side of the room, pretending to be working busily and unaware of the plan. When the room is ready, the second adult gives the final cleanup signal. At the signal, the children shout "Surprise!" and the second adult responds with delighted amazement.

"Trick the teacher" variation. Once the children have put the room in order, the first adult suggests that they might want to hide while the "unaware" adult signals the beginning of cleanup. The children then jump out and shout, "Surprise!" The "surprised" adult jumps up and down, joining in their excitement.

Chorus and verse — sing and clean. Choose a song that has clearcut verses and a lively chorus the children know (for example, "Jingle Bells" or "Bingo"). Begin the song and have all the children join in. Ask the children to clean up as adults sing the verses. When the chorus comes around, children stop and join in a lively singing of the chorus and so on until the room is clean.

Musical areas. Play a variation of musical chairs. Ask children to choose an area to clean. Put on music and ask them to begin cleaning. When the music stops, they move to another area and clean up there.

What's in my hand? Capitalize on children's love of surprises (and reinforce their developing comparison skills) by holding a toy in each hand behind your back. Have a child choose a hand — it is then the child's job to put away the toy in that hand. Children can also hide toys behind their backs for teachers or other children to choose and put away. You can also try this with contrasting pairs of objects. For example, the teacher might ask, "Do you want to put away the heavy thing or the light thing?" or use soft/hard, small/large, and smooth/rough pairs.

A cleanup challenge: "See how many things you can carry!"

In the "musical areas" strategy, children freeze when the music stops and move to a new area to clean.

Whisper cleanup. A fun and different movement game is to tiptoe and use low voices for a "whisper cleanup." You might open this cleanup with a made-up story about a big bear who is asleep under the house area table. The object of the game is to clean up the classroom without waking the bear.

Superhero cleanup. Ask parents to bring in old, cheap tee shirts. Cut off the sleeves and the fronts, leaving the neck fabric. Hand out these superhero "capes" and ask the children to "power clean" the classroom.

Simon says. Play Simon says, naming places that need cleaning. Occasionally add silly places that are not part of the classroom, for example, "Simon says, clean the doghouse" or "Simon says, clean the zoo."

Cleanup challenges. Challenge children to carry as many things as they can. Or encourage them to try balancing throw pillows or other objects on their heads while delivering them to the appropriate areas.

Race the clock. Set a kitchen timer or turn over a large salt timer for a predetermined amount of time. Challenge groups of children to clean up a specific area or a certain amount of toys (for example, all the blocks) before the time is up. Or challenge children to finish cleaning by the third repetition of the cleanup song. Challenge children to break their own cleanup "records."

"Race the clock" variation. Instead of racing a timer, play a piece of music and have children race to finish cleaning before the music ends.

Cleanup time doesn't have to be a tug of war between adults and children. When teachers and caregivers put aside unrealistic expectations and motivate children with planned activities and strategies that are fun, interesting, and full of choices, children are likely to be successful at cleaning up. Once they've experienced cleanup as an enjoyable part of their routine, they will be much more willing to engage in tidying up the room in the future — each cleanup experience is a building block that contributes to children's interest in participating and their general organizational skills. On a busy day in the classroom, it is easy to become too focused on the short-term goal of having a tidy room *that day*. If adults can stay focused on the long-term goal of developing cleanup enjoyment, personal responsibility, and organizational skills, they will plan cleanup strategies that sustain a sense of fun and purpose as children learn to take care of their play spaces.

Top Tips for Cleanup Time

- **Treat cleanup as a regular part of your daily routine,** giving it a 10- to 15-minute time slot.

- **Plan daily for cleanup.** Write the cleanup strategy for the day on your team plan. Your strategy may be based on singing, movement, pretending, symbol reading, or some other fun and engaging learning experience.

- **Use a wide variety of cleanup strategies,** changing them regularly, and posting them for quick reference.

- **Before cleanup begins, give children one five-minute warning or two warnings of shorter intervals.** When announcing the warning, tell the children what the cleanup strategy will be that day.

- **Use a warning signal,** such as playing a few notes on an instrument, turning the lights off and on, or starting a cleanup song, to indicate that it is time to clean up. Then begin the cleanup strategy for the day.

- **Structure the cleanup time so that it is a community cleanup.** Give children choices about where to clean up and what to put away; this may mean that a child will clean in areas he or she did not play in, and that other children will clean up the materials that child used.

- **Model a positive attitude toward cleanup.** Join in the fun, and be playful as you clean alongside children.

- **Expect the environment to be cleaned up to children's standards.** This may mean that some items are left out. Don't look for perfection.

Appendix —
Parent Resources

[Parent Letter Requesting Home Visit]

Dear Parent,

We are very excited about your child's arrival on the first day of school. We want to make sure this transition to school goes very smoothly for your child. We would like to make a home visit on____________. This visit is an informal occasion that we hope will give your child time to get to know his or her new teachers in the safety and comfort of your home. It also is a good time to ask any additional questions that you may have about our program.

Children react in different ways to this visit; some become very excited, some are very shy and quiet, some even run and hide! Whatever happens is okay with us. Just seeing us in your home will communicate our interest in your child and may help your child feel more comfortable at school.

During this visit, we may try to discuss with your child the choice of a "symbol" or "letter link," a special picture that will be used at school as an identification mark. These images are often pictures of favorite objects or activities. This symbol will be drawn by the teachers next to your child's name on artwork and where personal belongings are stored. "Picture reading" of such images supports growth toward reading and will also help other children recognize your child's materials.

We look forward to seeing you soon!

Sincerely,

The teachers at ______ Early Childhood Center

[This is a reproducible page.]

[Parent Letter to Accompany Handout on Separation Anxiety]

Dear Parent,

The start of school is an emotional time, full of anticipation of new friends, hopes for playful learning, and fears about your child's adjustment. Whether your child is returning to preschool or coming for the first time, he or she may experience separation anxiety. This a feeling of fear and discomfort about being separated from familiar people. Separation anxiety is a normal reaction that most people feel at one time or another. Adults experience it when they leave home and things are not the same. Unfamiliar stores, new and different ways of speaking, and foods that seem "foreign" can all can make us feel uncomfortable and anxious — no wonder McDonald's is the same from coast to coast!

Even E. T. (a movie character from outer space) suffered from separation anxiety. Despite the efforts of his newfound friends, E. T. still yearned to go home. E. T., however, had an advantage over most preschoolers. Although he was as frantic and upset as a 3-year-old, he had unusual electronic skills to cope with his homesickness (E. T. phoned home with a coat hanger, an umbrella, and an old record player). But young children have no such communication skills and their efforts at expressing their distress can be confusing and painful to watch and interpret.

Each child expresses these feelings about leaving parents in a slightly different way. Some children may protest right away, crying loudly at school or complaining at home. Some may complain of aches, pains, or illnesses. Others may have difficulty weeks after school has begun, when the initial excitement has worn off. Some children may show anger toward the new adults or children in their life.

It may help to remember that separating from home and becoming attached to new surroundings are vital parts of becoming independent. Children need our understanding and support as they make these steps. Enclosed is a list of suggestions that you can use to support your child during this transition. We hope you will find these strategies helpful and useful.

Sincerely,

The teachers at _____ Early Childhood Center

[This is a reproducible page.]

Making a Separation Plan

Leaving parents at the beginning of the school day can be difficult for any child, no matter how loved and secure the child feels. Here are some ideas you can use to make this transition smoother for you and your child:

- Help your child anticipate what will happen each day of school. If your child is returning for a second or third year in the program, let him or her know that there will be new children as well as some old friends in the group. Create a "separation ritual or plan" to follow with your child each day as you drop him or her off. Keep your plan simple (for example, a story together followed by a wave at the window or a few minutes together at the breakfast table). The teachers will be glad to help you decide on a ritual, if necessary.

- Be consistent about following your plan. If your child is having a particularly difficult time, adding "one more story" at the last minute will not ease these feelings; in fact, your child's sadness or anxiety may become stronger.

- If difficulties continue, reassess your plan with the teachers. Ask the teachers for suggestions and support — they have been through this many times with other children. Ask them what they do to support your child after you have left, making sure that your child's feelings are being fully acknowledged. Ask them what activities happen right after you leave so you can go over this with your child at home. (If you are still worried about your child after you leave, you can always call the school from your workplace to see how your child is doing.)

- Acknowledge your child's feelings yourself, both as you leave (if there are strong emotions) and at home when you discuss it. "Acknowledge feelings" means to make simple statements that label the feelings. For example, say, "It's really hard when we have to say goodbye at school. You feel really sad when I leave" or "It makes you mad when I leave you at day care." As you talk to your child, use a soft, calm voice and touch your child gently, to communicate that you understand. Pause and wait for your child's response. It is important to show you accept your child's feelings, even if his or her outbursts are upsetting to you. This acceptance will let your child know it is okay to have strong feelings about your leaving. With your encouragement your child will fully express feelings of sadness or anger — this usually helps children "let go" of the feelings and begin to adjust to the new friends and environment.

- If your child is not upset, avoid pressuring him or her to be sad that you are going. Instead know that your child cares very deeply about you and that you can take pride in your child's independence.

[This is a reproducible page.]

- Know that your child cannot begin to cope with your leaving until you actually leave. After your last goodbye, it is important that you leave without further ado. Children become confident that they are okay only after they have experienced their own ability to carry on without you in the new setting.

- Above all, show confidence in your child's ability to adjust by saying goodbye as planned. Do not sneak away while your child is distracted. This will make your child distrustful of the whole separation process.

Following these simple suggestions will ease this daily transition for most parents and children. If you need more help with separation problems, please feel free to talk with the teachers. We will help in any way we can.

[This is a reproducible page.]

Supporting Your Child at Pickup Time

On most days, arriving to pick up your child at the end of the program day is a happy, easy occasion. Your child has had a busy day and is eager to share what has happened or is tired and ready to go home right away. However, there are likely to be days when the transition does not go smoothly. Sometimes children are so engaged in a favorite activity that they refuse to leave. At other times, they may be so tired that they fall apart as soon as they see a parent. When your child is having trouble leaving, it may help to remind yourself that he or she — rather than being "bad" — may just need some extra support and flexibility.

If your child is resistant to leaving, take a few moments to notice a project he or she made or hear about something that happened that day. This can help your child adjust to the need for leaving and depart without an upset. If your child greets you by dissolving in tears, keep in mind that this doesn't necessarily mean he or she is unhappy at the setting or has had difficulties during the day. This outburst tells you he or she feels secure enough to "let go" now that you are there.

If your child is crying hard, give your full attention to his or her feelings by giving physical comfort and simply naming them: "You're feeling really sad." Avoid asking lots of questions; in particular, avoid asking the classroom adults if your child had a "good" or "bad" day. Your child's day has been filled with many activities — some may have been challenging and some have been fun and adventurous. When your child has calmed, ask the adults: were there any events today that are important for me to know about?

If you arrive to pick up your child and he or she is resistant to leaving, consider trying some of the steps listed below:

Six Steps for Solving Departure Problems

1. Be prepared for those times when your child is happily engaged and not ready to leave. When this happens, stay calm, and strive to be patient and see what is happening for your child.

2. Notice and name feelings that you see: "You are really having a good time on the swing." Or, "It's hard to leave when you've had such a fun day."

3. Observe carefully what your child is doing, taking in information about what is causing the departure problem. Ask the child about his or her activities. Say, "We need to leave soon. What's the problem? What's making it so hard to leave?"

4. State the problem from both your perspective and the child's: "We have a problem to solve — we need to leave soon, and you're having a really good time on the swing."

5. Ask your child to help solve the problem and be willing to negotiate in whatever small way is possible: "What do you think we can do to solve this problem,

[This is a reproducible page.]

since we do need to leave soon." Listen to your child's ideas. Be prepared to acknowledge feelings again: "I know you'd really like to stay for a long time, and we do need to go soon." If the child doesn't suggest an idea that can be negotiated, like "I'll swing two more times" or "Give me three more minutes," give a suggestion: "Can I tell you my idea?" Wait for your child to say yes — he or she will then be more apt to really listen to your idea. You might say, for example, "My idea is that we will sing 'Twinkle Twinkle Little Star' while you are swinging and when the song is over, we will leave. Shall we sing that song or another one?"

6. When you and your child agree on a solution, encourage and support this with a simple and enthusiastic descriptive statement: "Wow, we figured out the problem together! We each had ideas and now we've agreed on a solution!"

Sample Parent-Child Discussion

If departures are a persistent problem, discuss the difficulty you are having with your child's teachers and see if they have any insights. Then discuss the problem with your child in the morning or at the end of the day when your child is rested and not distracted by other activities (rather than during the departure time). The goal of the discussion is to give your child's feelings a thorough listening. The discussion may also result in a specific idea for a solution, but sometimes the solution is just that the child needs to know you understand what is he or she is feeling at these times.

The discussion might sound something like this:

(At a neutral time, not during pickup time.)

Jamie's dad: *(in a calm voice)* Jamie, I've noticed that when I come to pick you up at the end of the school day it's really hard for you to leave. Sometimes you become quite upset about leaving. What is happening for you? *(He pauses to listen for Jamie's description of the problem.)*

Jamie: Well, I don't like to leave 'cuz I'm having fun.

Dad: I am so glad that you're having fun at school. You really seem to like it there.

(They discuss what Jamie likes to do at school for a few more minutes.)

Dad: So it's hard when I come to get you, because you're still having such a good time and I need to leave quickly to pick up your sister. What do you think we could do to make pickup time easier?

Jamie: Let someone else pick me up.

Dad: But Mom is still at work, so there's nobody else who can come.

Jamie: Maybe I can have five more minutes.

Dad: Okay, five extra minutes of play time after I get there, then we'll leave quickly. That's how we'll solve the problem?

Jamie: Yep.

Dad: And, is there something we can do to make it more fun to leave? *(He pauses, waiting for Jamie's ideas. Jamie does not respond.)* Hey, I have an idea, do you want to hear it? *(Jamie nods yes.)* There are different ways we can go to the gate. We can walk to the gate holding hands and skipping, or we can race to the gate. What would you like to do?

Jamie: Let's race!

Dad: Yes, let's try that tomorrow!

[This is a reproducible page.]

Helping Your Child Get Ready for Kindergarten

How Children Express Anxiety About Moving On to Kindergarten

Children may express a variety of feelings after being informed that a transition to kindergarten will happen soon. Sometimes these reactions are surprising and/or intense. Some children will voice their worries clearly, but most will express their uncertainty indirectly, through changes in behavior. Here are some behaviors you may notice: increased sensitivity that results in more crying or other outbursts, interrupted sleep, night or daytime wetting, refusal to engage in outings and familiar routines, and/or increased demands for attention and reassurance. These expressions often occur at unexpected times.

As children contemplate the changes coming up, they may use intense verbal expressions, saying things like "I hate my new school" or "I hate my old school" (even though they have loved it all year!). This often occurs because they are trying to figure out how to shift their loyalties to the new program. Some children may begin to talk "baby talk" or engage in other "baby" behavior as the transition approaches. However disconnected or surprising such behaviors may seem, it is best to avoid comments like "You'd better not do that in your new school" or "That doesn't sound like a grown-up five-year-old." Such comments may only aggravate children's concerns that they may to fail to adjust.

What Parents Can Do

Whether or not your child exhibits any of the above behaviors, try these strategies to explore his or her concerns about the new school:

- **Discuss the upcoming changes at times when your child is rested and not distracted by other activities.** Avoid expecting certain responses or telling the child what you think he or she should be feeling about the new school. Listen carefully to whatever questions or comments the child makes upon hearing about the transition. Reflect back what has been said. For example, "It sounds like you really don't want to leave your school. It's been really fun for you there and it's hard to leave. What will you miss the most?" If your child makes a comment like "I hate my old school. It's for babies," you might say something like this: "You're feeling very grown up and ready to go to kindergarten now, aren't you? You are definitely not a baby any more."

[This is a reproducible page.]

- **If your child reacts to the upcoming change with angry outbursts or other immature behaviors, try to remember that these behaviors are not occurring because your child is being "bad."** Avoid arguing against statements about hating school; rather than being true, these statements are simply your child's way to express his or her feelings about leaving in an assertive and concrete way. Instead of hating school, your child may be overly excited about the change or, more likely, afraid. Simple comments like "You sound upset about the change. It can be scary to do new things sometimes" can help your child see that you understand. You might even tell a story about a time when you were afraid of trying something new and what you did that helped. Children often respond to such stories with ideas about what would help them. It can be tremendously reassuring for children to know that adults are sometimes concerned about changes as well and to hear that they managed them successfully.

- **Be patient and flexible in responding to your child's emotional expressions and behaviors, while still gently setting limits when they are necessary.** Things like dressing or getting to bed may take longer than usual. If the behavior is becoming more intense, you can make comments like "It seems like you're feeling upset and you really want me to give you extra help right now. Throwing clothes needs to stop. How about if I help you get dressed this morning?"

- **Give your child extra attention in any positive way possible, while also setting limits on any hurtful behaviors.** "It seems like you're having a very hard time today. Hitting needs to stop. When you're calmer, we can play a game or read a book together." These "acting out" behaviors often happen when children need to express something. Your positive attention shows your child you are listening. Rather than reinforce the unacceptable behavior, the extra attention you give will deeply reassure your child that you are going to support him or her through these difficulties. As a result, the hurtful behavior will very likely decrease.

- **Express confidence in your child's ability to make the transition; provide encouragement by giving specifics about the things that show he or she is ready for the new setting.** "Let's think of all the ways that you are ready for this change — you can put on your own shoes now, you can write the first letter of your name, and you even tell stories to your baby brother!"

[This is a reproducible page.]

References

Austin, J. (1999). *Fandagumbo* [CD]. Ann Arbor, MI: Author. Available from *http://www.julieaustin.com*

Evans, B. (Co-producer). (2003). *It's mine! Responding to problems and conflicts (Tender care infant-toddler series)* [Video and DVD]. Ypsilanti, MI: High/Scope Press.

Evans, B. (Co-producer). (1998). *Supporting children in resolving conflicts* [Video and DVD]. Ypsilanti, MI: High/Scope Press.

Evans, B. (2002). *You can't come to my birthday party! Conflict resolution with young children.* Ypsilanti, MI: High/Scope Press.

Gainsley, S. (2005a). Cleanup strategies from the Demonstration Preschool. In N. A. Brickman, H. Barton, & J. Burd (Eds.), *Supporting young learners 4: Ideas for child care providers and teachers* (pp. 91–94). Ypsilanti, MI: High/Scope Press.

Gainsley, S. (2005b). Cleanup time: What are those children thinking? In N. A. Brickman, H. Barton, & J. Burd (Eds.), *Supporting young learners 4: Ideas for child care providers and teachers* (pp. 83–90). Ypsilanti, MI: High/Scope Press.

Gainsley, S., & Lucier, R. (2001). Message board: A preschool communication center. In N. A. Brickman (Ed.), *Supporting young learners 3: Ideas for child care providers and teachers* (pp. 155–165). Ypsilanti, MI: High/Scope Press.

Healy, J. M. (1994). *Your child's growing mind.* New York: Doubleday.

Hohmann, M. (2002). *Fee, fie, phonemic awareness: 130 prereading activities for preschoolers.* Ypsilanti, MI: High/Scope Press.

Hohmann, M., & Weikart, D. P. (2002). *Educating young children: Active learning practices for preschool and child care programs* (2nd ed.). Ypsilanti, MI: High/Scope Press.

Lansky, B. (with S. Carpenter, Illus.). (1999). *The new adventures of Mother Goose.* Minnetonka, MN: Meadowbrook Press.

Pirtle, S. (1998). *Linking up* [Book and CD]. Cambridge, MA: Educators for Social Responsibility.

Ranweiler, L. W. (2004). *Preschool readers and writers: Early literacy strategies for teachers.* Ypsilanti, MI: High/Scope Press.

Schoenberg, J., & Schoenberg, S. (2005). *My bodyworks: Songs about your bones, muscles, heart and more!* [Book and CD]. Northampton, MA: Interlink Publishing.

Weikart, P. S. (Creative director). (2003). *Rhythmically Moving 7* [CD]. Ypsilanti, MI: High/Scope Press.

About the Author

Betsy Evans has been working in various roles in the early childhood field since 1974. She has been a program director, teacher, trainer, and behavior consultant. She is the script author and co-producer of the videos *Supporting Children in Resolving Conflicts* (1998) and *It's Mine! Responding to Problems and Conflicts* (2003) and is the author of *You Can't Come to My Birthday Party! Conflict Resolution With Young Children* (2002). She has presented trainings all across the United States, as well as in the United Kingdom, Ireland, Chile, and Mexico. Having experienced many everyday as well as extraordinary transitions in her own life, she has a strong appreciation for transitions that are planned well and are carried out with sensitivity and a sense of humor. Shown here, Betsy and her granddaughter, Zoe, amuse themselves during a transition with a rousing chorus of "Uncle Walter Waltzes With Bears" as they wait for family members getting ready for a party.